Career

Chameleon

Career Chameleon

One Life, Many Careers….
A Mind Lost and Found

By Ami Lauren

Published by Just Jhoom! Ltd
PO Box 142
Cranleigh, Surrey
GU6 8ZX
www.justjhoom.co.uk

Cover Design: Lianna Carnell
Cover Photograph: Ami Lauren
Author Photo: Lucy Fenn

ISBN: 979853 2847552

For those who want to make a difference in the world….
The dreamers and do-ers
It all starts with YOU!

At no time whilst writing this book did I want to cause harm or distress to anyone.
This is my truth.

Table of Contents

Foreword

Dance is in my blood. My first memory is that of being on stage at 3-years-old, in the very centre, surrounded by older girls, dancing. I was the star of the show – and I loved it! At 16, I went on to graduate in the South Indian classical dance style Bharata Natyam. But, when I decided to follow my passion in dance, I was told it was not a suitable career for a good Indian girl!

Oh - how I wish I hadn't listened to the naysayers. In 2010 at the age of 35, after having numerous careers including in hospitality, recruitment and advertising, I set up my own dance-fitness company Just Jhoom! creating a new form of dancercise that was inspired by the glitz and glamour of Bollywood. Drawing on a range of dance styles from classical Indian to salsa with dashes of hip-hop, jive and jazz, Just Jhoom! was seen as energetic, sexy, tongue-in-cheek, and a fantastic, fun way to keep fit! Over the course of six years, I trained over 300 instructors in the UK to teach it.

And this was how I met Ami. She describes in the book how we met at a dance convention, but my first real memory of her is at the instructor training weekend, when this smiling, enthusiastic young woman was so eager to learn everything she could. But, it was during the practical sessions that she really came into her own. Ami is a natural dancer, and she shines when she is dancing. Performance is in her blood.

So, when I read this book, it didn't surprise me that she spent so much of her youth on stage performing for people of all ages in a raft of different settings. What did surprise me, however, was just how many different talents she had. Aside from performing and teaching dance, Ami is a talented singer, accomplished magician and has had starring roles in pantomimes. What struck me about her story is just how adaptable she is depending on what she feels she wants to do, and what life throws her.

When Ami said she wanted to be on my new Pen to Published course and write a memoir about her life and the various careers she has embarked on, I was absolutely delighted. And when you read this book, you will see why.

Ami doesn't just tell us about her career changes and choices. She also shares her mental health struggles. Like all of us, Ami has had her share of challenges thrown at her in life, but rather than buckling under them she has faced them with stoicism and strength. At every crossroads she has reinvented and bettered herself, worked on her physical, mental, emotional and spiritual self – and has come out stronger and happier for it.

We sometimes think that we have to stay in one career for our whole lives. We are often told to do the "right thing" or be a certain way, often to the detriment of our own mental wellbeing. But this no longer needs to be our reality. More than ever, now is the time to follow our passion, reinvent ourselves and live the best lives we can. In "Career Chameleon" Ami shows us just how we can do that. Prepare to be inspired!

Shalini Bhalla-Lucas
Nairobi, 2021
@justjhoom www.justjhoom.co.uk

Introduction

During the second UK national lockdown in November 2020, I saw an advert from my friend Shalini. She was advertising a new course she was running, which was called 'Pen to Published'. Although I am no stranger to writing, I thought that it would be amazing to come out of the lockdown as a published author, so I contacted her and enrolled immediately. If you've bought this book, you'll know that I managed it!

Deciding what to write about was no easy feat. I knew that I wanted to send out a positive message, which would encourage people dealing with challenges in their lives with a simple message: "you can get through it". I decided to use my career path as the vehicle for this statement, as I certainly feel that it's been interesting and varied. I've learned lessons from every job I've had, and I carry the memories with me throughout my life.

If even one person benefits from what I have written, then my work is done. Regardless, I have personally gained an enormous amount from the writing process. It's been therapeutic to look back at different times in my life. I've been in contact with several friends, many of whom I hadn't spoken to in years, to talk through our tales. My life has been full of exciting highs and some pretty dark lows: probably just like everyone else's. We, as humans, love sharing stories though. Feel free to message me on Instagram @amilaurenpositivity to let me know if you've found anything in this book that you can relate to, or if it has spoken to you in another way.

I've learned through life never to miss an opportunity and to live it to the full. I know these are clichés, but we only have one life and we have to make it count. Your heart can tell you a lot, and you should follow it, no matter how crazy the messages you receive from it may feel.

As Dale Carnegie wrote, and my maternal grandmother (Bobe) always said, "Remember, today is the tomorrow you worried about yesterday".

Worries waste time, and I have experienced just how unproductive it can be to be consumed by them. Instead, we can all choose to live life right now, accepting and embracing every day that comes along.

My sincere hope is that you will enjoy this book and, amidst some serious topics, find it entertaining. After all, entertainment is in my blood...

Chapter 1 – Happy Feet

I never have, and probably never will, be able to match the feeling I get when I'm dancing on stage. I love to dance - the creativity, the adrenaline and the fun are intoxicating - but to have an audience increases the intensity. You have the pressure on you to get it right, especially when there are other dancers with you and you need to dance exactly the same steps at exactly the same time. Then, there's the applause. You're out of breath, dripping with sweat, but there's a massive smile plastered on your face and you feel it. The LOVE. That's the best way I can describe it.

My first experience of dancing in front of an audience was on stage at the Babbacombe Theatre, Torquay, aged nine. It was my first professional dance job in a show called 'Those Victory Days', which was dedicated to the musical and comedic heroes of the 1940s. I loved everything about it: the costumes, the other children who were as passionate about dance as me, and the adult cast members who inspired me. Plus the fact that once a week I got paid two pounds to tap dance on stage! Back then, it felt like a fortune, and it made me feel special: none of my school friends had jobs. Tap has always been my favourite genre of dance, possibly because I like the opportunity to make lots of noise, but also because I'm from a musical family background and I can sense the rhythm in my feet. I thought I was destined for stardom. The only part I didn't like was my Mum poking about with my face to get my makeup on and off.

Since then, I've had many other dance jobs, but to this day I can still remember the routines from that show. Grandad has a grainy, shaky video that he puts on occasionally and I dance along. They say you always remember your first. Well, that stage was definitely where I found my first love.

My audition was nerve-wracking. I sat at the back of the dark auditorium while several children went through the steps on stage, one group at a time.

"Do you think I'll get it?" I asked Mum.

"That's up to the choreographer", she replied, "You won't just get the job because you're my daughter". As the only child of a well known illusionist and the granddaughter of local entertainment agents - I always felt I had to work harder than everyone else to prove myself. Luckily, I still shone and got the part on my own merit. I don't think I've ever got used to auditions, but they're just like job interviews really: designed to give you nerves and butterflies in your stomach, full of tension that can either give you incredible energy or break you. I was lucky that my first audition was so positive; it didn't always end up that way.

I come from a family of entertainers. Mum was a dancer, actress and 'Anna Merlina', Europe's leading lady illusionist. Even now, she still performs children's shows under the new name of 'Anna Banana'. Mum knew that dance training was a great platform for any child to gain confidence, coordination and make friends, as she had been through it from a young age too. With this in mind, she sent me off to the Marisa Burgoyne School of Dance, aged three. Her parents, my grandparents, were well known mind readers and mentalists, years ahead of their time. They performed shows and stunts across the South West of England for several years, appeared on television shows, then retired from the stage to become light entertainment agents. I didn't get to know my biological father well, but I remember him being a talented musician and going to watch his band play at local holiday camps when I was very young. Both my half-brothers have natural musical ability, mine manifests itself in my feet and through my voice.

I'd see Mum going off to work at night, her big brown eyes heavily framed with multicoloured powders and lashings of mascara, her lips painted bright red. She had short brown hair back then, but she'd put on long, curly wigs to make herself look larger than life. I remember her leaving the house looking spectacular from the neck up. Since she had to carry huge props in and out of venues before she got into her stage costumes, she would wear an old brown jumper with holes in it, leggings and boots. I adored her and thought she was the prettiest lady I'd ever seen. She had several glamorous assistants over the years too, who I enjoyed spending time with and who often rehearsed at our house. Between rehearsals they would play with me or do my hair and makeup, as if I were a real-life Barbie.

It wasn't just human performers. We had two miniature poodles, Muppet and Genie, who were used in the magic act and were thus very well-trained. Genie passed away when I was five-years-old, but Muppet, who had become part of the family just before I was born, was my best friend until I turned 15. Mum tells me stories of how protective they were of me, and how they would growl if people in the street tried to look in my pram on walks. We also had some magic doves that lived in an aviary in my grandparents' garden, but they would come into the house to rehearse and fly around the big downstairs hallway.

Whenever Mum retired a dove we would get a new one, often a hatchling born in the aviary. Sometimes she would let my brothers and I name them, which is how we ended up with Stormbird, Blackeye and Mrs Frisbee.

My grandparents often doubled up as babysitters for me. Grandad, a larger-than-life Cornish man with a big smile and a toupee, was a little bit too loud for my liking when I was a small child. Strangely, considering how close we have eventually become, I would hardly say a word to him when I was small. On the other hand my Bobe (pronounced Bubba, the word for grandmother in her native Yiddish,) was my favourite person to hang out with in the world. Bobe had big brown eyes and dark hair like my Mum, always wore a big welcoming smile and gave a soft hug. We would watch musicals and sing together, she'd watch me dance and let me have 'discos' in their lounge with the lights off while Top of the Pops (my favourite TV programme) was on. I know the lyrics to thousands of songs as a direct result of singing the days away with her.

We always had a steady stream of showbiz visitors, who would drop by both our house and my grandparents' when I was little. 'Trot', nicknamed from the Dame character he played in pantomime, had a strong singsong northern accent and was Grandad's best friend and drinking buddy. Adam, the comedy impressionist with his ventriloquist puppets - Orville and Nookie Bear - lodged with us for a while and built up a strong bond with one of our dogs. The 'Stage Door Johnnies' regularly tap danced through our door, smiling, singing and joking frequently. Barry Manning, one half of 'The Mannings' was a small man, but looked large and round in the plethora of costumes that he was dressed in for the quick-change, comedy and dance act he performed with his wife Fiona. Tim Pope, a loud and large character, marched around in a 1940s costume ready for a themed show. Finally, the acrobatic twins Spencer and Lee would arrive in their costumes on unicycles, juggling anything and everything they could get their hands on. It all added up to create an incredibly fun childhood for me.

My family all have a strong work ethic, based around the show business mantra of 'the show must go on'. I remember Mum hobbling through her act on a broken foot. My grandparents were both working away on different pantomime productions when I entered the world. If you were ill or grieving, you still went on stage. It was all about reliability and trust – you didn't let the rest of the cast down, or the venue that had booked you. Recently, when Grandad was very sick in hospital, I asked a friend to stand in for me in a show, and Grandad did not approve. As an adult, I've kept my family's work ethic with me and I would never let anyone down if I could help it. Despite this, I also think it's important to remember that physical and mental health must come before any job.

Around the time of 'Those Victory Days', I had started competing in the local Paignton Dance Festival.

When I won the Modern section the first time I entered, I was extremely proud of myself. I had worked really hard with Miss Marisa to practice and perfect my routine, and eventually it all paid off. Mum and Bobe were in the audience that day clapping and cheering. I entered a couple of ballet sections too, dressed in a pretty tutu, as well as the song and dance sections. In these I used costumes and props from Bobe's production shows to enhance my performances. I loved playing dress-up in her costumes and was lucky that Mum's friend Carol was on hand to take things up and in for me to make them fit.

I can still remember the scene. The curtains open to reveal the stage set with a colourfully painted jukebox, a backdrop of big records and a life-size pink Chevrolet. The lights come up, dry ice fills the stage and a three-piece Rock 'n' Roll band, 'The Hi-Tones', launch into a lively medley. Full-skirted dancers spring onto the stage, followed by leather-clad vocalists. This was the exciting opening to the second professional production that I took part in, the 'Rock Rock Rock' show. Mum had asked me and two friends from dance school if we'd like to be involved in the show, which she had produced, for £12 per night. Obviously, we jumped at the chance. By this time I was able to do my own makeup, which was hugely beneficial for Mum and a lot more comfortable for me too. The show started in June 1997 and continued throughout the Summer. I would rock up in my school uniform, then transform from 'little Ames' (Mum's nickname for me) into a dancer. Delia, Danielle and I would gossip backstage about boys and school and lots of silly things that all seemed incredibly important to us at the time. The choreographer was a bubbly lady called Suzy, who was also in the show with another adult dancer called Kathryn. Suzy somehow managed to break her leg half way through the season, so there was a shuffle around with spacing and covering some of her parts. Then Kathryn also dropped out of the show, but she was replaced with the ultra-lively red headed Lisa, who we had so much fun working with.

Delia and I were also tasked with promoting the show by handing out leaflets on Torquay seafront to the many holidaymakers. We would hand them over with winning smiles and invite the recipients to come and watch the show - with the leaflet they got a discount on tickets. As a new venture for my Mum, she wanted the show to succeed, so naturally we did too. I remember Delia getting awful sunburn from walking around the seafront without the right sun protection, then a naughty, 11-year-old me slapping her on the back and causing some real pain!

Once the summer season had finished, Mum asked Delia and I to perform some routines with the vocalists and the 'Hi-Tones' for a showcase she had set up to bring in some extra work for artistes in the area. Delia and I were happy to do so and spent time running through the routines to the new, ten-minute medley of songs we were to perform. On the day, the songs were played at double the speed we had rehearsed, and we simply had to speed up to stay in time. I'm still unsure of how we got this so wrong, but luckily things went to plan and subsequently we were engaged to perform at a couple of social clubs in the South West that winter.

My next audition came the following spring. A vocalist and producer 'Debbie T' was looking for a dancer for the 'Around the World' show at the Rainbow International Hotel in Torquay. I went to watch the show with Mum and loved all the different styles, from Can-can to American Trilogy. We had a chat after the show and Debbie acknowledged that, although 12 was still very young to be working in a venue with a bar, I looked older and we'd possibly get away with it. I auditioned privately, got the part, and started rehearsals. These were with Debbie's daughter, Jo and Kelly the choreographer, in one of the function rooms next to the swimming pool in the hotel, which always smelled of chlorine when we rehearsed. Jo was a couple of years older than me, tall, with long, shiny dark hair, dimples and a constant cheeky grin on her face.

"Ami, why don't you do this?" she'd say, encouraging me to cause some mischief. Such was her nature, it was always difficult to know if she was being serious or winding me up, but we were constantly joking around and laughing together.

The night of my debut performance in the show was so exciting. I had wanted to do the Can-can since I'd first seen it, and now, here, I was ready to go out in front of the audience. The first number in the show was 'Copacabana' and we were dressed in gorgeous jewelled bikinis with feather headdresses. There were several quick changes in this show, which was a new thing for me, but I loved the costumes and managed it all well with the help of Jo and our other troupe member, Leanne. After the show, Debbie dropped me home and I was too excited to sleep.

I performed in the 'Around the World' show one or two nights every week for just over a year. In that time I became great friends with Jo and Leanne, who were the first to properly introduce me to the equine world. Although Bobe had taken me to rescue centres and farms to meet horses and other animals when I was younger, I'd never been particularly hands on with these magnificent animals before. Debbie had a few horses, one of which Leanne loaned from her because she and Jo would ride them in shows at weekends. I started going along and helping with the horses – learning to muck out and groom at the yard, and then attending the shows with them on a Sunday morning after a Saturday night performance. Some Saturdays, we'd stay overnight at the yard in the horse box so we'd be ready to go to the show the next day. My favourite was Georgia: a young horse being brought on by Debbie at the time. I loved grooming her and leading her around. Debbie also took me out on rides, during which I'd normally go on Jo's horse, Crystal, who was the calmest of the group. This was good, because I wasn't the most confident rider and I have always preferred my relationship with horses on the ground, however, I went along on hacks with the other girls. I was never quite safe from Jo's pranks: she once told me to ride a small pony bareback, as apparently he was very calm and it would be easy. I mounted, then fell off backwards almost instantly!

I felt lucky to have my friends and show business interests outside of school, because, at the time, secondary school was no picnic.

It wasn't as if I wasn't academic or didn't like school. My primary school years had been fantastic. I enjoyed my education and was always ahead of the class: I'd be asked to help other students to read and solve maths problems. I took my textbooks home with me and would work through as many of the comprehension puzzles or sums as I could each evening. In the end, the teachers started running out of pieces of work to give me.

I sailed through my 11-plus exam and gained a place at Torquay Grammar School for Girls. Mum and a couple of assistants from her illusion show had attended the school themselves, and they told me they had enjoyed their time there. I started as an eager, optimistic 11-year-old. Thanks to three years of bullying, I finished it in a very different place. I'll never be entirely sure of why I was picked on, but I think the reasons behind it were that I looked older than I was: I'd already developed breasts by this time and my period had started, which my main perpetrator didn't seem happy about. I think she wanted to be the most 'grown-up', which I find ludicrous, as having a period has never seemed particularly exciting to me. I did have a few spots, which I suppose most teenagers do, but never full-on acne. When I look back at photos, you can hardly see the blemishes, but kids are cruel and my complexion earned me the name 'cheese grater face'. As much as I loved going off to dancing classes or to appear in shows after school, I think this also created a bit of a divide between my peers and me. They didn't really understand what I was talking about when it came to my life outside school, or why I was never available for sleepovers.

In the shows I appeared in, there were always adults around working or performing with me and I was used to socialising with them. I also had some financial independence, as I was making good money even then. Perhaps I grew up too fast: at the age of twelve, I was already smoking and drinking to fit in, simultaneously trying to blank out the horrors of the school day, where I'd be called names or tripped up in the corridor.

"Mum, I can't go to school any more. You have to take me out. I can go to a different school," I cried to her one day as I came in from school and threw myself on our staircase.

"Baby, I'll do everything I can, but surely you can talk to a teacher? Someone at the school can do something?"

"They can't. They haven't. I hate everything and everyone".

I was no longer eager to do school work. I lost interest and wanted nothing more to do with the place. Mum spoke to my form tutor who said she'd look into it, and perhaps she did, but nothing changed. She also told Mum I'd been caught smoking behind the school and asked if I had an eating disorder, as I never went into the canteen. (Actually, I would always eat in my classroom in a corner to avoid the bullies.)

The teachers just didn't see or understand the hell I was going through.

Chapter 2 – Magic and Mayhem

I was born on New Year's Eve, 1985. A few days after the event, there was an article in the local newspaper featuring a smiley me, held by Mum, who was wearing her full stage sequins. The headline was *'Baby Amy is Magic'*.

Magic has been a huge part of my life since the very beginning. There were props and costumes stored in our house and rehearsals took place there frequently. My older brother David and I would sometimes dress up in Mum's feather boas and wigs and make illusions out of cardboard boxes, then perform them for all the family. We had no idea that this didn't happen in everyone else's houses.

On New Year's Eve 1992, my step brother Ben (my Mum remarried when I was six) and I had our first opportunity to assist Mum with her act, on stage at the Torbay Hotel. Ben hobbled around the stage with a prop walking stick as 'Old Father Time'. He then jumped into a box shaped like a doll's house. Mum closed the box, spun it around, and when it opened he had vanished. She closed it again, then out of the roof popped me, 'Little Miss New Year'. There was another photograph of Mum and me in the paper to celebrate this occasion.

Mum also performed magic at children's birthday parties and events. This was a completely different show, in which she would dress in a colourful, floral two-piece suit and create mayhem with puppets called 'Hog the Dog' and 'Roly the Rabbit' alongside a range of clever trickery. She normally took one of her assistants along to be a character called 'Aunty Big Nose', who would join in with any cheering, hissing and booing and get the children to play along. Muppet the poodle featured in this show too, and afterwards the children were able to stroke her as she was a calm, happy dog who lapped up any attention she could get. Mum would take me and sometimes my brothers along to watch the shows, and we never tired of watching and shouting along with the audience. We also particularly liked the lollipops and sweets she gave out as prizes; she would tell us that if we were well-behaved while she was working, we could have one after the show. She used to perform a great trick with two pieces of tissue paper, which magically transformed into a hat with the help of two children from the audience; one boy and one girl. She would rip up the tissue paper, roll the pieces into a ball then ask them to "give the pieces a magic blow!"

Then she'd open up the tissue paper, now a hat, and place it on the girl's head. When she told her it was for her to wear at her wedding to the boy, it always prompted a lot of laughter and often the girl would protest wildly! They'd be rewarded with lollipops for taking part though. Later on in life, when I performed my own magical speciality act, I performed this trick too. It was low-maintenance and inexpensive, but it always got a great reaction.

I loved being 'the assistant' and took every opportunity I could to try and learn some of the secrets to Mum's illusions. They were closely guarded of course, even when it came to family members. She couldn't risk telling children who could pass the information on to their friends at school.

Mum wasn't a member of the 'Magic Circle', but she was part of the 'International Brotherhood of Magicians' and had won their coveted 'Craig Trophy' at the age of 17. She took magic extremely seriously; it had always been her passion and career. She had learned the tricks of the trade from Grandad when she was in school and would perform in talent shows and school concerts under his watchful eye. He had also been a young magician, who had forged a successful career in magic after being given a simple conjuring set for Christmas. He was told by his family that he could not make a career out of show business, and that he was foolish to think he could perform magic as anything but a hobby. He was born into a traditional Methodist family, many members of which actively disapproved of his trickery at the time. Luckily, my grandfather didn't listen and became very successful as a magician in his own right, part of a mentalism double act with Bobe, a main character in several pantomimes, and a tutor to Mum when she decided to perform.

When I was 13, I finally got the chance to be her assistant, as her previous one had taken on a new job. She decided that I was old enough to go on a year's tour with her before she retired from performing. I was super-excited and spent time after school and at weekends rehearsing, until the day finally came to perform. We had some regular shows in some of the local hotels, went to various Haven and Pontins Holiday camps and spent some time on the Isle of Wight. Mum had let me choreograph some of my own dance pieces for the show too, which was still my favourite part of performing.

It wasn't always easy working together, possibly because of the close relationship that we had. If we'd had an argument that day, which was usually over me not wanting to attend school, I would do ridiculous things to get back at her on stage. On one occasion, a 13-year-old me was hypnotised and floating in the air with Mum standing below, presenting me with her arm up. Then, I gave her a bit of a kick. She got her own back once though, almost setting me alight inside the 'cage of fire', an empty box from which I would emerge through the flames.

"Come on Ami!" Mum would shout to me as she loaded the props into the van after the show. Normally I was busy chatting up boys, and I got quite a lot of attention from them too. Part of this was because I was on stage, more probably to do with some of the costumes I was dressed in, including my PVC playsuit! I was also now at the age where I was noticing boys more, which was not helpful for poor Mum. However, sometimes one of them would then offer to help with the lifting of our heavy illusions, which worked in our favour overall.

The van was a big, white Toyota Hiace, and we managed to fit everything in there perfectly, leaving no gaps, like a crazy jigsaw. On the way home, to keep Mum awake, we would play loud music through the old tape player in the van and sing along. I was particularly fond of the Alanis Morisette 'Jagged Little Pill' album, and I remember Mum trying in vain to sing loudly over the swear words. We would have picnics of crisps and chocolate in the van, or sometimes, for a special treat,

Mum would buy us hot chips from the holiday centre cafe. I was a fussy eater, by now a vegetarian, so my chips had to be entirely plain with just a small sprinkling of salt.

By this time we also had a new addition to the act and our family, who would ride up in the front of the van with me and sometimes fall asleep cuddled up on my lap during those late nights. Wizzo the Maltese Terrier was picked up at a service station in Wales following a fun family holiday to Butlins Minehead in 1995. Muppet, the poodle, was getting old and needed to be retired from shows, and a friend of Mum's had recommended this breed as a great dog to train. It also made a bit of a change from the poodles. From the moment we picked up Wizzo, we all fell in love with this tiny, white ball of fluff. She was quiet for most of the journey home, sat between Ben and I in the back of Dad's car.

Then suddenly we heard a tiny "Uff!" It was a noise we would become incredibly familiar with over the next 15 years.

Wizzo was not the same on stage as the poodles. For a start, she was not as graceful, and she also had a fiery temper. The poodles would exit the box they had appeared from, give a little shake, stand tall, prance around the front of the stage, then go off wagging their tails. Wizzo, on the other hand, would come out of the box poised for a fight, run to the front of the stage, growl fiercely at the audience, then run off barking. The lesson we learnt here was that if you are going to use a dog in a magic act, don't use a terrier! Wizzo was fun to be around and was a very pretty little dog. She loved the family and was incredibly loyal, but to the point where both the postman and the window cleaner ended up with holes in their trousers thanks to her efforts defending the house.

I would not encourage people to use animals for entertainment nowadays, neither would Mum, but at the time we didn't know any better and several other magicians were using animals as part of their act. The animals we shared the stage with were always treated incredibly well and became part of the family at home. A few years after we had stopped doing the show, Mum got her props out to get them ready to be sold. Wizzo became very excited upon seeing the box she used to appear from, which I think shows that she secretly enjoyed her time in the spotlight!

Mum's oldest dove, Eric, was at least 30-years-old when he passed away. We had moved him in to the house from the aviary at this point, as he was our last surviving dove and we wanted him to feel warm and be near to us. Mum had a special relationship with Eric and was distraught when he eventually died.

Growing up with animals in the house and working with them definitely helped to encourage my love of animals in general. I learnt to respect them from a young age, and my dogs were always my closest friends.

I was really sad when we stopped performing the illusion act, but Mum was ready to move on to the next stage in her career. As for me, I had two years to get my act together at school and try to scrape through my GCSEs. I'd attended school as little as possible due to having tonsillitis, pretending to have tonsillitis because I didn't want to go, and being on tour or sleeping off a late night of magic. Mum kept the illusion props for a few years before selling them, in case I felt I wanted to take over the act at any point. I didn't though, "I want to be a dancer, not a magician."

"You'd get more work performing magic. There aren't many female magicians around," she responded. At that point I was adamant that I'd be going to stage school and then performing in musicals or on 'Top of the Pops' as a dancer for the rest of my life.

Eventually she sold the props, as they were taking up a lot of room in our shed and gathering dust. It was better that someone made use of them than them rotting away.

School improved. I met my best friends in year nine. Actually they were always there, but I'd just kept my head down so much due to bullying for the first couple of years that I didn't speak a lot to anyone. I'd sat next to Melissa a couple of times in year seven, and she was a really sweet girl, but very quiet. She often sat alone, reading or looking at school work, so I approached her one lunch break and we got on really well. She had made friends with some other girls in our class by this point, but they were all in higher sets than I was. I was in the lowest set as I'd fallen behind so much, so I didn't really know them. They were all very clever, and often I had no idea what they were talking about, but I enjoyed having some company. They also didn't really 'get' what I did after school with my shows, but they were polite enough to listen. I persevered with forming relationships, started to have some fun with them, and we are all still best friends to this day.

I also formed some friendships with girls in other tutor groups, who realised that I looked older and carried a confidence about me that enabled me to buy cigarettes and alcohol from local shops. Suddenly, the days of being bullied were behind me: I was celebrated and given money to run these errands so that they too could indulge.

My parents let me go out clubbing with some of my friends who also looked older, under the proviso that they, or my friend's parents, picked us up at 11 p.m. We made sure that we were always on time to be picked up, no matter what fun we were having, so that we didn't lose this privilege. However we had also taken to pretending we were at each other's houses so that we could stay out later and go home with some of the older people we had grown to be friends with. Luckily we were safe, but I feel awful looking back on some of the lies we told our parents in our teens!

I became increasingly self-conscious in my mid to late teens. I'd had to battle the bullies earlier in life, which put me on edge about any spots I got. To counter this, Mum and I picked out different skincare solutions and my GP put me on some tablets for them.

In addition to this, my two top front teeth looked somewhat dull and discoloured, to the extent that you can hardly see me smiling with an open mouth in any photos from back then. I went to the dentist, who told me it was due to acid from fruit juices wearing down my tooth enamel. He told me he could fit veneers across the front of my teeth, and as I was under 16, I got these done on the NHS dental scheme. When I had the veneers they felt strange at first, as they were something foreign and felt big in my mouth, but I soon got used to them and started smiling again.

My hair was also a difficult topic for me. Mum had neither the patience nor the knack that other dance mums had to plait it beautifully, so the responsibility was often left to my dance teacher. I felt it was frizzy and messy, and Mum would constantly produce a brush to drag through it in an attempt to improve the look. I had it dyed for the first time, hoping for a beautiful light blonde colour, but instead it turned grey, which encouraged more ridicule at school.

Perhaps these are trials that every teenager goes through in some way. I took it all to heart. I was desperate to be the prettiest girl, because maybe then I'd be liked.

Chapter 3 – Dished Up

Apart from dancing in the 'Around the World' show, Jo waitressed at The Rainbow Hotel part-time to pick up some extra cash.

"It's really easy and I get a lot of tips, especially when people recognise me from the show," she said.

Mum was happy about me getting a job as she felt it would help with my independence and teach me more about finances. I decided that I'd give it a go, and despite my age, the restaurant manager offered me a couple of trial shifts when they became short staffed. It was a huge restaurant as the hotel accommodated around 250 people when full. We would be busy serving in different sittings for around three hours for breakfast and dinner, then there was all the laying up and cleaning down that needed to be done before and after meals. Several of us worked there, including many foreign staff members who were accommodated in the hotel quarters. There were plenty of young people on gap years or working shifts around college too.

I was dreadful at the job. I was tiny, so lifting trays full of heavy plates or cups was not ideal for me. I'd often be branded as 'lazy' by the grumpy chefs, or I'd drop things. As a vegetarian I hated serving plates laden with meat and taking away messy leftovers. I couldn't pronounce some of the names of the fancy meals and I got laughed at. However, Jo was right; guests loved me and my personality, especially the ones who recognised me from the show.

"How long have you been dancing?" they would ask, slipping me a fiver and telling me to live my dreams and keep up the good work.

Whilst working at The Rainbow as a waitress, I met one of my good friends, Sonia, who it turned out was a couple of years above me at my school. Sonia was great, simultaneously good fun and very down-to-earth. She helped to show me the ropes and, as a girl of five-foot-three herself, was able to give me some tips on carrying the heavy trays. We started spending a lot of our weekends together, mainly going on nights out trying to get into clubs underage. We'd stay at each other's houses, go on holidays together, and I even dated her brother for a short period of time. Unfortunately, as she was in a different year to me at school, I was unable to see her much there, but it was comforting knowing that she was around and I could find her if the bullying became unbearable. She was also a lot more confident when it came to standing up to the grumpy chefs. I hadn't developed much of a thick skin at this point, so when they shouted or were sarcastic towards me, I'd invariably end up in tears, whereas she was able to banter back with them. Soon I started to get the hang of it, but I still wasn't keen on the chefs.

I worked there with Sonia and Jo for a good couple of years, during which time I saw many staff members come and go. We mainly worked weekend shifts because of school, but we would help out more in the summer holidays. I couldn't do many evening shifts though as I had dance classes three nights a week, shows on a couple of nights and homework to do. One summer, a few of my colleagues were renting rooms at a house with a swimming pool around the corner from the hotel, so in the break between breakfast and dinner, we'd all go back there to hang around the pool, sunbathe and swim. Some of the guys would chuck beer into the pool to cool it down and then we'd go diving to retrieve it. I was loving life: I made good money for a kid, had grown up friends and the weather that summer was amazing.

I'm not sure why I eventually left The Rainbow, it was probably due to a fall out with a chef, but shortly afterwards I landed a job at the hotel next door, The Cavendish. This had a smaller restaurant, and I didn't know anyone there, unlike The Rainbow where I'd known most of the staff from my time doing the shows there. It was a family-run hotel and everyone was very friendly. I instantly made friends with Candice, who was a couple of years older than me and also working her shifts around school. She showed me the ropes and we had a lot of fun together. The chefs at The Cavendish were a lot less cantankerous; in fact the head chef was always smiling, unless his football team had lost. He was more reserved and understanding during my first few shifts. The second chef was a younger man with long hair, which was definitely a big plus for the 14-year-old me, possibly due to the teen-pop heartthrobs at the time, Hanson. He asked me if I'd like to go for a drink one night and we ended up dating for the rest of the summer. I'd also go on nights out with the rest of the waiting staff, to comedy clubs (which I hadn't explored before), and live music venues. I really enjoyed my time at the Cavendish, but before long I ended up in my next waitressing job at The Tormohun Hotel.

The Tormohun was a smaller hotel again, also family-run. The owners were a couple called Ray and Jean, who both smoked as if it was going out of fashion. This was a time when you could still smoke indoors, and I remember now how Ray would greet me from behind reception, dark glasses on, dragging on a cigarette,

"Good evening Ami," rasped a dry voice.

The Tormohun guests varied in numbers. In the summer, it was very busy and we'd be a staff of four or five each day, whereas out of season they normally only needed one or two of us to work. I'd find out whether I was needed from week to week. In the summer, they sometimes had shortages of other staff, so they asked me to try my hand at housekeeping once. Let's just say they didn't ask again after that! However, the owners did find something else that I could do: Jean was fascinated by my stories of dancing and I would sing around the hotel while setting the tables.

"You have a lovely voice," she told me.

At the time, I was in the school choir and was attending private singing lessons with our music teacher at school. It was my dream to attend stage school at some point in the next few years, so I needed to be able to sing and act as well as dance. Jean came up with an idea.

"Ray has an old PA system. How about we set it up and you can do some singing for the guests?"

I was delighted at the opportunity and at their belief in me, so Mum put me in touch with one of her contacts who made backing tracks. Soon I had put a little half-hour set together to perform for the hotel's audiences. Similar to the Rainbow, the guests enjoyed seeing one of the employees turn their hand at something else, so I got lots of compliments and extra tips.

The Tormohun was sadly getting quieter and quieter. A couple of the others on the waiting staff told me they were going to a busier hotel, The Devonshire, and asked me if I'd consider moving with them. I seized the opportunity and said goodbye to Ray and Jean. They understood, and they closed down completely not long after.

The Devonshire Hotel was another large hotel that stood on a hill in Torquay, looking out over the sea. Waiting service here was a little different to the other hotels I'd worked in. There were no trays, so I had to learn (quite quickly) to carry several plates in one hand without spilling any gravy. I have some of the smallest hands most people have ever seen, so I was never going to be able to carry more than four at a time, but I soon got used to this. I also tried my hardest to manoeuvre myself towards tables for two so that I only had to carry two plates and a vegetable tray at a time. Occasionally, The Devonshire hosted silver service events. I wasn't especially good at this and invariably sent potatoes flying. On these occasions, I generally offered to do something else, like fill up water jugs.

The owners and managers loved to host different parties and events, so from time to time we would get to play dress up, which I always had fun with. At New Year's, I particularly enjoyed dressing up as a tramp with my ripped jeans and shirt, topped off with fake dirt all over my face. It was great fun and the management tended to reward us all with drinks in the bar when we'd finished our shifts.

After food service, the guests could move their chairs slightly to face a little stage at the end of the restaurant, where a singer or musician would play for their entertainment in a bay window. There was a small dance area too, if they chose to get out of their seats. The restaurant manager, Nigel, called bingo before the entertainment started, and I found this amusing, particularly as I'd worked in entertainment venues with bingo before. I'd never been able to call it previously, as I'd been under 16. It wasn't Nigel's favourite part of the job, but it was something I really wanted to do, so I suggested to him that he let me have a go. I think he was cautious at first, but gave in and hovered over my shoulder in case I called the wrong thing or got nervous. I called in perfect diction and the audience enjoyed the little jokes I threw in between games. I was a natural entertainer, so Nigel soon left me to my own devices with the bingo machine.

I was 16 now and in my GCSE year at school. I'd already dropped out of Technology, as I was really behind in classes and it wasn't my strongest subject. I was in the bottom sets for Maths, Science and English, and had chosen German, Art, R.E. and Drama as my options. Mum tried to steer me toward my academic work, but I was always happier dancing and earning money at the weekends, and she couldn't exactly lock me in the house. I also found it difficult to sit down and concentrate for long periods of time, so when I did study I tended to do it in blocks of about an hour. I drew spider grams or used coloured pens so things stood out to me as memorable. I had chosen to stay on at Torquay Grammar School for Girls to do my A-levels, not because I especially enjoyed it there, but because we lived a convenient ten-minute walk from the gates. Between periods and at lunch times in year 11, when we were supposed to stay in school all day, I would often sneak home. Mel and my other friends were staying on at the school too, so I would be able to avoid having to make friends all over again or risk being bullied. To be able to stay, I needed to attain certain grades though, which according to my teachers was no sure thing.

"It's always the quiet ones..." my Maths teacher would say, as I had a nap on my desk during algebra. Sometimes she'd shout at us collectively, "You're all getting 'E's!"

On other days she'd try a different tactic and persuade us to do our work by promising homemade Mars bar cake if we did. We really loved that.

When it came to the exam days, I was actually quite nervous. I stood with my class mates outside, chewing on a pencil until it was time to go in and sit at my allocated desk. I made sure I wrote for the duration of every exam – I certainly had things to say, it just came down to whether or not I was writing the right things.

My German oral exam was hilarious. I had a short German teacher, who we often hid the whiteboard rubber from on top of the board, knowing he couldn't reach it without standing on a chair. I wasn't that bad at German, or at least I could get away with it. I'd been on our school's German exchange trip in year ten and had a whale of a time. My oral exam was different though. Perhaps I cracked under the pressure, but the words didn't seem to come and my long-suffering teacher had to help me by gesturing with his hands and mouthing words frantically while the tape recorded.

Once the exams were finished, I had the extended summer break to forget all about them. I concentrated on working at The Devonshire, dancing (as I was also taking my advanced exams in Modern and Tap), and clubbing with my friends. By this point, my parents seemed to have given up on curfews and I had a mobile phone, so they could call and check I was safe. I painted the town many shades of red with a motley crew of waiting staff members and school friends. Several of the bouncers knew me in the pubs and clubs in town, and I'd not had much trouble getting in to them for a few years anyway because of my confidence. There was a pub at the top of town that I frequented from time to time, mainly to win their karaoke competition on Sunday nights. On one occasion I had the nerve to go in there wearing my school uniform with just a Kappa jacket over the top. No-one batted an eyelid.

I was also developing my singing skills and wanted to enter a local summer talent competition, 'Stairway to the Stars'. Mum recognised that if I was going to perform in the theatre for the competition, then I needed to get used to singing in front of audiences. She introduced me to Nigel Lee, a fantastic local cabaret singer who offered to take me to his gigs with him so I could practice in the middle of his act.

"Here's a young lady who has a bright future in show business. Let's give her a big welcome and some encouragement. It's Ami Lauren..." he would say, and the audience would applaud as I strutted onto the stage.

I practised my set of three songs ready for the competition, wearing a stage outfit that consisted of a long, shiny red dress with feathers at the top. This could be whipped off using a Velcro strip down the side of it to reveal a shorter, silver dress that I could dance more freely in. I had a good laugh with Nigel and he was very kind to me. When the day of the talent show came, lots of my friends and family piled into Torquay's Riviera Centre to watch me perform. I was nervous, as it was the first time I'd sung in front of such a big audience, but also excited for the opportunity. At just 16, I was one of the youngest entrants and while I didn't get through to the next round, I did get some inspiring responses from the judges that helped me improve my performances in the future. There is never failure, only feedback!

Finally, the day came to collect our GCSE results. At the time, it felt like the day that decided our future, and as I stood with Mum in the entrance hall of the school, I suddenly wished I'd studied harder. Then, my name was called out and I collected my envelope. I grabbed Mum's hand to pull her to a corner of the hall, away from my classmates, who were either celebrating or commiserating. I opened the letter at last and found I had somehow managed to get two 'A's, three 'B's and four 'C's. I hadn't failed anything and I would have my place in the sixth form. I jumped up and down and hugged Mum tightly. She had tears in her eyes.

"Well done! Now, let's go and celebrate! You've earned it".

We spent the rest of the day having a girly shopping trip in town and food at a pizza place on the harbour. It was nice for someone to serve me for once instead of the other way around. Apart from one more, short-lived waiting job at a Pirate-themed Caribbean restaurant when I was 18, my dishing-up days were thankfully about to be over.

Chapter 4 – Bingo!

In year ten, we had to find a work experience placement. As the only thing I really wanted to do with my life long-term was dance and entertain people, I was lucky that Mum had some contacts and she helped me arrange something suitable. As my classmates set off to their nine to five jobs in accounting, law, the zoo, the library, a museum or a shop, I went to Beverley Park Holiday Centre. I spent a week on the entertainments team: most of my hours were worked in the evenings, but I had some daytime duties with the kids club too. In the day, I helped to judge or referee sports tournaments and poolside competitions. Then, in the evenings, I called back the bingo numbers to the caller when someone made a claim, encouraged people on to the dance floor for party dances and helped keep the children away from the stage when the live cabaret acts were performing.

During work experience, I stayed with my friend Stacey, as Beverley Park is in Paignton, the next town along from Torquay. Mum said it was too far to take me back and forth every night, especially while she was working. I enjoyed staying with Stacey, as I felt like I was having a little holiday. In the daytime I worked on the presentation I would have to give about the work experience placement when I arrived back at school.

I enjoyed the week immensely and obviously made a good impression too. The entertainments managers invited me back to work there a couple of days and nights a week throughout the summer. I learnt a lot more over this time and grew into my assigned responsibilities. I always helped to run the poolside competitions and I had become more comfortable on a microphone, so I'd sometimes talk through the rules with people, then adjudicate and give out prizes or award points. I helped with the table-tennis tournaments too, which sometimes got quite heated! In the evenings, I put on my makeup and one of my favourite dresses, then a colleague would pick me up for work. I would help with the children's competitions and games, dance with guests through the evening and help the team get props and costumes ready for their shows. I rehearsed a couple of songs with the resident band that I sang with from time to time, which was a real highlight for me. It didn't feel like work at all, as it was so much fun.

When I was 16, Mum told me about a position that would be coming up locally at The Tor Park Hotel. The entertainment host was going on maternity leave, so cover was needed. The job would involve calling bingo, running a nightly quiz or game show, building up the cabaret act and putting them on stage, then running the end-of-evening disco. I was keen, so Mum put me in touch with the entertainments host and I spent some time shadowing what she did and learning the ropes. Of course, I'd had a go at calling bingo during my time at The Devonshire Hotel, but now I had the huge responsibility of selling tickets and the organising of prize money too. It might sound simple, but I can assure you that when you have a long queue of guests wanting books and a short amount of time in which to calculate, things can go wrong!

On Monday nights, a local dance school came to the hotel and the children performed for the guests. Their music was all on tapes, so throughout their performance I would have to constantly change tape for each child's music. The guests loved watching them though, and they had some lovely costumes including beautiful tutus. For the rest of the week, I would have various singers and comedians appearing as the evening's cabaret. I worked four nights a week at the hotel; the other three were covered by musicians who would try and get the guests up dancing all night.

There was a lot of responsibility placed on my young shoulders in this role, as the entertainment for this hotel and all their guests, who were mainly in the 60-plus age bracket, was almost solely in my hands. I rose to the challenge, helped when needed by management and the bar staff. We all worked as a great team and also socialised a little bit after work. The manager would let us all have a drink or two from the bar when the guests had gone to bed, and we would chat and laugh until the early hours. Sometimes the cabaret acts would stay behind to chat too, and I'd often manage to talk them in to giving me a lift home so I wouldn't have to pay for a taxi.

The Tor Park Hotel operated on an all-inclusive basis for the guests, meaning that they would normally drink a good amount of alcohol before the bar closed at 11 p.m. Some of the guests drank responsibly, others did not, becoming red-faced and slurring by the evening's end. I vividly remember one evening, when a man came into the bar from dinner, already quite tipsy. He told me that he and his wife had been for lunch at Wetherspoons that afternoon. They sat on a table near me at the front of the stage to watch our visiting cabaret for the night, a fantastic performer called Al Diamond. Al was a wonderful Welsh-man with a great singing voice and some fun stories and jokes up his sleeve too.

"There was an Englishman, a Scotsman and an Irish man..." he began.

"I won't have him being rude to the Irish," the drunk man next to me slurred.

"He's just telling a joke," I assured him.

"No, my family are Irish and we won't be made a mockery of!"

Before I knew what was happening he'd heaved himself to his feet and wobbled over to Al who was performing in the centre of the dancefloor.

"My family are Irish and I won't have you talking badly about the Irish!" he told Al, who looked very uncomfortable.

Another man, who'd had one too many himself, then also stood up and declared, "Sit down, it's a joke."

"I will not sit down," said the man and went to throw a punch at the other man.

Al moved back from the dancefloor and the bar manager came over to usher him out the back entrance of the room. I ran to the reception to find the night porter, who doubled up as security. He and the hotel manager came into the ballroom, where a fight was now in full flow involving several guests. They took hold of the initial perpetrator and removed him from the ballroom. This broke everything up and the guests returned to their seats. The bar manager told me to turn everything off, as there would be no encouraging them to stay and drink more that evening. The man's wife, who was still at the table next to me, got up looking embarrassed and left. I was quite shocked, everything had happened so fast. It was also quite unexpected, especially with a performer like Al who was very politically correct, warm and likeable. It shows what the effect of alcohol can be on someone, even on those well into their 70s.

The next evening, when I arrived for work, the hotel manager told me that the man had been locked in his room and left to sober up overnight. He'd then come down for breakfast looking sheepish, remained quiet and stayed out of people's way since. I really felt for his poor wife: I'm sure that was not quite the holiday she was hoping for. He was quiet in the ballroom that evening too, but he did come up and apologise to me eventually.

Working at The Tor Park Hotel, I continued to sing where possible and had quite a nice selection of tracks after my initial performances at The Tormohun Hotel. Sometimes guests would suggest songs that might suit my voice, so I'd go away and look them up, then if I liked them I would order the track and learn it. I normally performed on a Monday after the children had completed their dance show.

I had a range of quizzes prepared as well, from general knowledge to a 'getting to know you' quiz, in which the audience had to guess true or false in response to a number of statements about me. I used the 'Mr and Mrs' game show, in which couples are tested on their knowledge of each other, and played a version of bingo in which everyone had a number and danced along to music. If it was your number called, you had to sit down and the last person left standing won a prize.

When the entertainments hostess came back at the end of her maternity leave, I was sad to leave the hotel. However, as it was part of a chain of hotels in the local area, I was called upon to cover holidays and absences from time to time. Despite being part of the same chain, each hotel was slightly different in the way that they operated and what was expected.

The Torbay Hotel, on Torquay seafront, was the largest of the hotels I worked in. Unlike The Tor Park, this hotel did not run the all-inclusive deal and was a little bit more upmarket. It had a large ballroom floor and most of the evening, apart from bingo and cabaret, was taken up by ballroom and sequence dancing. The regular hosts there were normally musicians who could play for dancing, but when I covered I muddled through as best I could with MiniDiscs. The Torbay was also open to non-residents, so several locals who enjoyed dancing would attend nightly to get their fix. I became very friendly with a couple called Sheila and Gordon, who taught me to ballroom and sequence dance. As a natural dancer I picked it up relatively quickly, but being led is very different to dancing solo. I made sure I danced with them, sometimes with others, once I'd got the hang of a routine, whenever I was at the hotel. The Torbay became my favourite venue to host at for this reason.

I was not as keen to sing at The Torbay because it was so much bigger than what I'd been used to. I was asked if I could partner up with a keyboard player as a duo for some Sundays while the regular host had their day off. This appealed to me more, as we could banter and I'd have someone to share the stage with. Steve was very skilled on the keys and also taught me some harmonies so that we could sing together. The guests enjoyed what we performed for them and they danced all night long.

On some occasions, Mum organised for me to travel with a cabaret so I was able to host at the hotels further away from Torbay. I spent one Christmas, as well as many other occasions, at The Imperial Hotel in Exmouth, which was a big hotel with a small, relaxed entertainment room. I enjoyed this hotel because I could get to know most of the guests who came in to watch. We'd chat about where they had come from and what they were doing on their holiday. I liked making them feel special. It also meant I was able to tell any visiting cabarets about the personalities in the room, so if they were planning to invite someone up on-to the stage I could recommend who might join in.

Once a year I attended an entertainment host seminar, which was usually held in Torquay in the off season. Mum conducted a lot of the training as part of her role booking entertainment for the hotel group. It was lovely to meet entertainers from all over the country, hear how they ran things differently and to share ideas with each other. We'd go on nights out when training had finished and cause all sorts of mayhem in the town. I made friends with several of the hosts and went to visit them in all the different locations. James worked at the Shearings hotel in Pitlochry, Scotland, and I flew up to Edinburgh to meet him. I enjoyed watching him work in the evenings and exploring the sights and tea shops of the Highlands during the day. While there, we also took a trip over to a hotel in Oban and saw how another host,

Claire, ran the evening entertainment. I visited Paul in Eastbourne on a few occasions and always learned a lot from him: especially seeing his colourful costumes and passion for the lighting rig. Everything he did was meticulously planned to ensure the greatest entertainment value.

From working on an entertainments team and as a host, I realised that talking to people, with or without a microphone, is something that I can do naturally. I tend to be able to conjure up some conversation topics and put people at ease very quickly. I wasn't the most confident person though. Some evenings, even in the hotels I knew well, I felt nervous when a new crowd arrived and I had to make new connections again. I'd worry that they wouldn't like or warm to me, or would view me as a little kid, especially at the beginning. Somehow though, I would just get through and do it and we'd all have a fun night.

I ended up working for The Shearings Hotel chain on and off for close to twenty years, first as a host, but later as a cabaret act and as part of a duo. I loved every minute of my experience with them, and was incredibly sad to hear that they went into liquidation during the 2020 coronavirus lockdown.

It goes to show that nothing in life is certain, so it's good to have many strings to your bow....

Chapter 5 – Capital Eye

I completed my 'A' levels alongside a weekend job at Boots, on the pharmacy counter. I learnt a great deal about medications for minor ailments and completed my Healthcare Assistant training course. I've always loved learning in a practical way and helping others, so I enjoyed being able to study, watch more experienced staff members in action, then give people advice about their health and wellbeing. I didn't enjoy the warehouse or stacking shelves quite so much, but as with everything in life, we sometimes have to accept the rough with the smooth. I constantly find myself reminding people that we wouldn't know happiness if we didn't know sadness, and we wouldn't know good if it wasn't for bad. Stacking shelves was a very shallow example of that. I was still working as an entertainments host at weekends at the time, as well as clubbing with friends regularly to try and spend all the money that I'd made. Not just this, but I'd be dancing at Marisa's on weekday evenings. Let's just say the two years were very busy ones.

During a trip to London for an event my Mum had put together (where I was meant to be helping out but mainly chatted to people and got drunk), I met my first serious boyfriend. He worked for an entertainments agency in the city and was good fun. He started coming down to visit me on weekends and we'd go out for dinner and drinks whenever I could fit him in around my various jobs.

In the midst of all this, I was auditioning for different stage schools and courses, as I'd decided that after sixth form, this was what I wanted to do. Mum regularly travelled with me to London for auditions, but I was getting worn down by every "no" I received. It's such tough competition in the dance world, especially if you need to get a scholarship or grant, as we couldn't afford the fees any other way. However, I then saw an advert in The Stage newspaper for a course that really caught my eye, titled *'Diploma in Popular Music'*. The course description explained that I would have the opportunity to write music, take singing and commercial dance lessons, learn how to work in a studio and record my work. It was a one-year course, attending the school two days a week.

It seemed perfect. I'd been writing songs for fun since I was 12-years-old and had a book full of ideas. Mum and I travelled to Nottingham so that I could audition, and there I sang a pop music track and danced in my favourite style, rather than performing musical theatre as I had done at every other audition. I felt a lot more comfortable with this than I had at the other schools.

"Why this course and not our Musical Theatre course, especially with your background?" asked the principal. I explained that I was passionate about writing music and wanted to work in the popular music industry.

Looking back, I should have expressed my interest in the three-year, full-time Musical Theatre course. It might actually have been better for me, but I was thinking about my relationship and getting some free time with my boyfriend, as well as working to support myself while I was away. I would say I regret it, but I believe you choose your path in life and learn the lessons you're meant to. Eventually you'll end up where you are meant to be.

I received a notification to say I'd passed my audition a couple of weeks later and I was excited about starting. I was also over the moon to be able to tell my teachers at school, who had been nagging me to apply for university placements, that I'd secured a place doing something I actually wanted to do. The Grammar School expected everyone to finish their 'A' levels and go to university, although the motives for this were unclear. Often it felt like they wanted to be able to tell the world that a percentage of their students graduated to higher education, but how many people aged 18 really know what they want to do and choose to study something worthwhile? This was a year of my life that would be devoted to exploring my love for music and dance, and I felt happy about that.

I passed my 'A' levels in Philosophy, Psychology and Drama, with an 'A' and two 'C's, then finally passed my driving test at the fourth attempt. I packed all my belongings into my second-hand Nissan Micra and moved to East London the day after my test, to first enjoy a long summer holiday living with my boyfriend.

Having worked for Boots, a nationwide chain of pharmacies, for two years, and with glowing references from my managers, I'd decided that I would easily find a job in one of their many branches in East London. Sadly, things weren't quite that simple. I went from store to store, handing over my CV, only to be told "Thank you, but we aren't recruiting right now".

I spent my days wandering around the docklands area looking for opportunities in shop windows and scouring newspapers. I came across some employment agencies and signed up to a couple, hoping that I'd have more luck with them than I had on my own. This turned out to be the case: within a couple of days I'd been called by 'Office Angels' and invited to an interview and typing test with them at their Canary Wharf office. The company was eager to have me on board as an administrator and offered bits and pieces of work at different placements in Canary Wharf. This was the life, I thought.

The work itself wasn't overly interesting, but I got to sit in offices wearing smart clothes, using a headset to take calls, writing notes and typing letters, and looking out over the Thames or watching the general hubbub of London life. I was better paid than I had been before, probably because I was in London. I saved up the money I received, then splashed out to watch musical theatre shows in town once a month.

One day, I took a call from someone at the agency who asked me if I'd like to interview for a more permanent fixture. This was successful, and I became an employee of Platform Home Loans for the rest of the summer. There were a few other temps from Office Angels working at Platform too, and it was just down the road from their office anyway, so every Friday we'd get together for lunch as a social opportunity. I started off at Platform as all the others did: stuffing envelopes for seven hours a day. This was as mind-numbingly boring as it sounds and I hated it: I got constant paper cuts and developed a burning hatred of sticky labels. I smoked a small amount at the time, and we were allowed to go outside for cigarette breaks, so I'd go out every hour to break the monotony.

I got to know my manager at an after work drinks event at the pub across from the office, and soon I plucked up the courage to ask if there was anything else I could do.

I told him how intelligent and skilled I was and that I was wasted stuffing envelopes. He gave me a chance doing some data-input work: I'd enter the details of mortgage applicants into the system, which would generate a positive or negative result and details of how much they could borrow. This was much more interesting, so I stuck with it until it was time to start college.

Mum and I had visited Nottingham once since my audition, and we'd even found a place for me to stay, with a lovely older couple whose children had flown the nest. I'd be staying there with one of the other students from my course for two nights a week while I attended college, then going back to London for the rest of the week. I got on well with the other students, and a few of us would hit the town in Nottingham for the wildest nights out that I'd ever experienced. When you get a group of dancers together, there's no fun like it. A particular highlight was a club called 'Flares', a 70s-themed club that was part of a chain. We'd go there every Thursday to compete for the 'Dance Idol' trophy and a bottle of free sparkling wine. One of us would win every week without fail.

On the school side, things were not much fun. It was the first year that the college had run the course and they seemed to be having some teething problems. The singing and dance tuition was incredible, and I learnt skills there that I've never forgotten, but the production and business side was not as well put together. The teachers from those subjects had their own gigs to fulfil, which often caused them to be late or tired in classes. One by one, people started dropping out of the course and eventually, after a term and a half, I followed suit.

I'd also been having problems in my relationship. I was 18 and he was in his mid-20s, looking to settle down. I wasn't ready for that, and I missed my home town too, especially the sea. One day while he was at work, I packed everything up into the Nissan Micra and moved back home. I called my Mum on the way, explaining the situation in tears. She, thankfully, was calm. "Concentrate on your driving. We'll deal with everything else when you get home."

Upon arrival at my parents' house, Mum cooked dinner and cuddled me as we talked through it all. She also answered the phone to my confused boyfriend, who had arrived home that afternoon to find me and all of my belongings gone.

As luck would have it, the lodger in my parent's granny flat, just behind the house, was moving out at around this time. I needed my own space, having lived away for seven months, so they allowed me to rent it at a low cost. Mum also gave me a temporary job, helping her with administration in the entertainments agency, which she had taken over from my grandparents when they retired. I started hosting again on certain evenings too, back in the local Shearings Hotels. I relaxed and enjoyed life at a slower pace: London and Nottingham had been fun, but the weekly travel and transitions between college and work had tired me out. The daughter of a friend of Mum's, Jayann, also worked in the office. We'd always been close, ever since she was born, and we were happy to spend time together in and outside of work. We would go to watch the acts that the agency booked and enjoy nights out together dancing on podiums in various nightclubs.

By this time I had lots of backing tracks, which had accumulated during my stints singing at The Tormohun, hosting, and studying in Nottingham. I practised my singing each day, and had realised that this gave me more opportunities to perform than just being a dancer. I told Mum that at the next round of auditions she held, I would like to perform a short selection of songs to see if she felt I would be up to scratch as a cabaret vocalist.

There is so much more to being a cabaret artiste than just singing, a lesson that had been drummed in to me for years. Alongside your voice, it is equally important to have good stage presence and rapport with the audience, dress properly and make a good impression with the management at the venues you perform in. Luckily, I had honed these skills to a great extent during my time hosting. The day came, and Mum held an audition at The Torbay Hotel one afternoon. I performed, and she was impressed by how far I had come. She agreed to give me a contract to sing as a cabaret act one night a week at The Imperial Hotel in Exmouth, where I'd previously hosted. I knew it well, so it was the perfect place to get used to my cabaret set. My act went down well each week at the hotel, and Mum received good reports from the management and host, so she started booking me into other venues too.

It was not easy for Mum, as a well respected agent, to book her daughter to her clients. A lot of them knew me from various events, so she couldn't exactly hide who I was. Our family ties put additional pressure on both of us for me to be a great act, because if there were any doubts, she could lose a client. Still, I proved myself time after time and several venues asked for me to return, impressed by my quick costume changes and dance, as well as my natural ability for putting an audience at ease. Her confidence in me grew, as did my confidence in myself, which led to me working not only in the hotels, but in some of the bigger holiday parks in the South West too. These included Haven Holidays, Park Holidays and the John Fowler Group. At the parks I was able to sing more modern material, which I loved.

All in all, it was a successful couple of years. Then a big opportunity came knocking. One I couldn't say no to.

Chapter 6 – Life's an Act

An illusionist called Steve Waller, whose career was really taking off, was on the hunt for an assistant. Mum asked me if I'd like to do some shows with him, and I jumped at the chance, having enjoyed assisting her so much when I was younger. Steve was a fun, easygoing Geordie who, alongside his wife, taught me what I needed to know. I worked with him for a couple of weeks in Scotland, before he got an exciting call.

Mum had submitted a video of his act to the producer of Q'dos Pantomimes, Jon Conway. Jon wanted to include Steve in his summer tour of the Haven Holiday venues, performing in pantomime during the day, then as part of a variety show in the evenings. The cast was made up of three cabaret acts, who formed the variety show, and five dancers, singers and actors who came together with them for the pantomime in the day. I was really happy for Steve, but sad too, as it meant I wouldn't be able to continue performing the illusion act alongside him.

However, although I didn't know it at the time, Mum had also submitted some footage of me to Jon Conway, and it turned out that I'd been accepted on to the South West tour as part of the cabaret team too. This was a huge opportunity – at the time Q'dos were the biggest pantomime providers in the UK, and I knew that if I impressed, it could potentially open a lot of doors for me.

The two other acts I would be working with were a comedian, who had worked for Mum for a considerable time, and a comedy impressionist who had also worked for my Grandparents before they had retired, so I knew him well. Both of them were under Mum's management, so she pushed them to get a place with Q'dos for the tour. I was sent a script for the pantomime 'Jack and the Beanstalk' in which I was cast as Fairy. I went over the script every day and practised with Mum and Jayann. I also recorded it on to a tape, which I listened to in the car on the way to gigs and before I went to bed at night. I was taking this opportunity very seriously.

In March 2006, I travelled up to Scarborough with the comedian from my team for our rehearsal week. There were several tours taking place across the country, and we all met up there together. The dancers, singers and actors who made up the rest of the cast for the pantomime had arrived a week earlier, as they were to be performing a pirate show and a couple of other shows at the parks during each week. There were so many people present that I felt quite nervous and self-conscious. What if I couldn't keep up? All the other cabaret acts had been doing this for a lot longer than me, but I kept Mum's advice in mind.

"See this as an opportunity to learn and grow," she told me, so I promised myself that I would take in every bit of information and feedback that was passed on to me.

Rehearsals for 'Jack and the Beanstalk' went well. We'd start at around 9 a.m. and go on until 5 p.m. when we'd go off to make dinner, then join up with the rest of the team for drinks. I tried not to get too involved with the drinking culture, as I wanted to be on the ball for rehearsals, but it was hard not to when everyone was so involved in drinking games and fun each night.

When it came to the last day of the week, we had final dress rehearsals for the pantomime. The seamstress and Jon's mother, Wynne Shearne, had a stock of costumes and props from the countless years of productions, which were stored in a big warehouse. We visited this at the start of the week, and once a costume that suited us was found, her team would make the necessary adjustments.

"What part are you playing?" she asked, as I approached the warehouse.

"Fairy in Jack and the Beanstalk," I replied, proudly.

"I have just the thing," she said, flashing a sparkling smile and a wink.

I followed Wynne around the numerous rails until she came across the most stunning purple and gold gown I had ever seen.

"This costume was made for Letitia Dean when she played Fairy for us," she told me, referring to the successful 'Eastenders' actress.

I tried the gown on. Although it had a corset top and ribbon to tie me in, it was too big and too long.

"Don't worry my beautiful fairy, we can fix this!" Wynne ushered over a colleague, who measured me and took away the dress to be altered. I was also presented with a sparkly tiara and some New Yorker shoes, which weren't particularly glamorous but were great to dance in.

By the time we got to dress rehearsals my fairy gown fit me perfectly and I felt every inch the part.

For the variety show, Jon had given us instructions to get together with the other two members of our team to start generating ideas. Although we were great individual acts, he wanted a few sketches or songs in which we all came together to make it more of a show. I spoke to the other two acts about it after rehearsals, and I wasn't greatly reassured by their plans to "throw something together nearer the time." I'd always ensured I rehearsed well for every performance I did, because this meant I could perform to the best of my ability. I didn't want to feel unprepared, especially because the show was due to start in a couple of weeks, but I had to remind myself that these people were more experienced and had been doing this for years. Perhaps I needed to chill out more.

I returned home utterly exhausted, but looking forward to starting the tour. We were covering the Haven centres in Weymouth and Poole; four venues in total. We did not have accommodation provided, but each centre had what they called a 'cabaret van' which was essentially a caravan put aside for visiting acts. We were told we could use these to relax in between shows and sleep there if there was no other need for it. I also agreed with Mum that I'd continue to perform my cabaret a couple of nights a week too, as bookings were still coming in for me around my tour dates.

It got to the day before the tour started, and I'd still not heard from the other members of my team about our variety show. I was pretty anxious, and Mum agreed with me that we shouldn't be leaving it so late, so I called the comedian who I was working with. He said, "Let's wing it for the first night. We'll have loads of free time together after that to put something together properly. Bring your tracks and you can sing a few numbers in each half of the show."

I felt uneasy as the instructions from Jon had been to put together a show, but I couldn't do anything about it.

The next day I got up early, feeling a mixture of excitement and nerves, and headed to Weymouth. I was the first person to arrive at the park, so I waited in my car until I saw the Mercedes Sprinter van, which contained our scenery, props and costumes, pull up with the comedian in the driving seat. We all helped him unload. We had got to the venue early in order to do a run through and sound check on the stage. This went well, and although there were a few teething problems with our headset microphones, we found that if the entertainments team at the park turned off their devices, ours worked perfectly. After the run through, we got into our costumes and put on our makeup for the first show, then had a lot of fun performing it. My favourite part was singing with 'Fleshcreep', who was the baddie in the pantomime. There was also a particularly fun part in which one of the cast dressed up as Jack's cow and did a dance. The children in the audience reacted perfectly to this, and it was certainly a highlight.

After the pantomime, I went to get some food with the other two variety show cast members, and we talked through how the show would be structured. We would take it in turns to do a 15-minute spot, then there would be an interval, then we'd do the same again. With one of the comedians there was an opportunity for me to bring on some of his props so we'd look more involved with each other, and at the end we rehearsed a walk down and bows to some music. It wasn't what Jon had asked for, but it would work for the next few nights while we settled into a routine with the pantomime and got to know the parks. Then, we'd work on some other bits together, they told me. I was happy with the situation in the meantime and the show went well that night. The audiences were getting three cabaret acts rolled into one, so I expect it seemed like great value to them. Fortunately both of the comedy entertainers were extremely talented and great at getting the audience participating and laughing along.

The show stayed like this for the entire seven month run. I asked several times whether we should turn it into more of what we'd been asked to do, but was told that while it was working really well and if there were no complaints, everything was fine.

Jon came to see both shows and seemed pleased with them. He asked for a bit more interaction in the variety show, but as the entertainments managers and guests alike were happy, we only changed a few small things.

I made lots of friends in the parks that summer. There were some lovely 'Haven Mates', band members, and most of our team were lovely too. I say most: I almost pulled out of the production that August after months of bullying from one of the cast members, who would constantly tell me I wasn't good enough.

"You only got this job because of who your Mum is," he'd say, which was not only hurtful, but untrue too.

Mum had sent in my video along with all the other artistes' showreels and Jon had chosen me without knowing who my mother was. For all I knew, he still hadn't made that connection.

"Your voice isn't great. Any of the Haven Mates could do your part." Perhaps they could, there were several very talented entertainers on the teams, but I'd spent time building up my act and was only performing a snapshot of that in the variety show.

"You're so ugly. I have friends who are models and they wouldn't even stop to look at you," was another hurtful and unnecessary comment over lunch one day. I'd started feeling self-conscious about my teeth again, as my veneers from my childhood had become a bit wonky, and when one cracked, my dentist had just patched it up. I decided that with the money I'd saved from doing the shows I would go to a private dentist and get them done properly, which helped somewhat with my feelings about my appearance.

I took it all and tried not to show my feelings, walking away from him wherever possible. However, the final straw came when he started talking badly about my mother, the very person who'd helped him, managed him and got him this opportunity. She'd known that the bullying had been going on, but I called her in tears and said I needed to leave the show.

"Ami, you can't do that. It's a professional contract. You have two months left. You must do whatever you can to get through it."

So I did. My boyfriend at the time, a magician who was also working hard in the South West, would come and stay with me when he could so I didn't feel so alone.

Other times I'd stay with some of the Haven Mates I'd made friends with. The bully would say, "You shouldn't impose yourself on them," but that wasn't what I was doing: they had offered and we enjoyed each other's company. I'd begun to question myself a lot, and unsurprisingly my confidence had nose-dived. Even when you know someone is saying something just to get a rise from you or upset you, it doesn't mean you don't take it to heart. I was feeling sensitive. If I pointed out to him that he was being irrational or saying nasty things, he would laugh and say he was just winding me up, but I can assure you that it didn't feel that way. I got through the last couple of months as best I could, and as much as I'd loved the shows and the experience, I was happy to be out of it by the end.

I went home and spent the winter singing in local hotels and helping out in Mum's office. That New Year's Eve I turned 21, so I treated myself to holidays in Egypt, Italy and Florida during 2007 to celebrate. I'd only ever been as far as Tenerife previously, and these experiences gave me quite the travel bug. I especially loved Egypt: the history and culture were fascinating.

In February 2007, I attended the Blackpool Magicians Society Convention with my mother and grandfather. We had several associates who were also attending, including my boyfriend and some other speciality cabaret artistes who Mum had booked over the years. I loved the convention so much – I never realised how many magicians there were in the world and the shows each evening were incredible. In the daytime, we would attend lectures, workshops and roam the 'dealer's dens', where tricks and props were sold. It felt like a real-life world of Harry Potter. Even when the shows finished in the evenings, the bars were open all night so we could socialise and drink through until the early hours. I met several well-known magicians from all over the world, and all of them wanted to show me or teach me tricks. Realising how varied and fun the world of magic was suddenly ignited a flame in me, a desire to perform it, despite having told my mother previously that it wasn't for me. There were hardly any women in magic, as she'd told me, and I felt I could really find a niche within the business. I still didn't want to do illusions, but I thought some of the pretty, clever trickery could be quite fun and decided to start exploring further.

Around the same time, Mum started talking to a magician friend in London called Richard Leigh. Richard was producing a big show in October and wanted some dancers, illusionists and magicians to take part. They discussed how he would be keen to develop and produce illusions and acts for other performers. I expressed my interest, along with a couple of other acts, and started working with Richard with a view to performing in his show. The goal was to have our own magical speciality acts ready for the 2008 summer season.

Next, Mum received a call in the office from a pantomime producer called Tony Peers. He was looking for a fairy character to perform in 'Snow White' at the Spa Theatre, Scarborough that winter. He asked if she knew someone suitable. Mum told him about my experience with Q'dos and also mentioned that I'd be able to bring a magical element to the show. He loved the idea and asked for a showreel to be sent. Luckily I'd been able to put something together with Richard Leigh to add to my vocal, dance and acting reel. We sent this to Tony, who promptly contracted me for the pantomime.

When I was offered a part in the next Q'dos tour that summer, I didn't have to think twice. I knew that I'd been unlucky with the cast the previous year and that this year could be very different. The team was to be structured differently – rather than a cabaret cast and separate singer/dancer cast, there would be one team of six for each area. The area I was offered to cover this year was Devon, Cornwall and Somerset, which suited me perfectly. I could stay at home most nights, and it would be a shorter tour anyway, just two months to cover the main school holiday period. As it happened, I was cast with a couple who I already knew, as they worked for Mum frequently and I'd been on some nights out with them. I didn't know the other members at the time, but I looked forward to meeting some new people and having some fun experiences. The pantomime this year was to be 'Cinderella', and I was given the role of Prince Charming. Initially I was quite unsure about this because of my high voice and small stature. However, Mum had played this role in her youth and I decided I would get some tips from her and take on the challenge. As it turned out, our Cinderella was even tinier than me, so it worked out well and, as an added bonus, made the ugly sisters look like giants. We would also be performing a pirate show that year which sounded like fun, so I worked hard on my script, as I had done the year before.

Rehearsals were held for a week in July at the same venue in Scarborough. I got on very well with the other cast members, who seemed more focused and motivated than the cast I'd worked with the year before.

My Prince costume from Wynne's team was a sparkly, gold and silver tunic. I wore my hair up for the role which gave me a more masculine appearance and added to the illusion that I was taller.

I travelled to Scarborough and back with a performer I knew from rehearsals the previous year, who had been cast on one of the other teams. Our journey back was horrific, as the river Severn had burst its banks and the M5 was flooded. We ended up staying overnight on the motorway, going to the toilet in an empty water bottle and sleeping under our coats to try to keep warm. When I finally got home I felt exhausted and ill. I stayed in bed for a solid 48 hours, sleeping, eating and watching TV with my faithful dog Wizzo by my side.

A week later though, we were on tour and I was loving life. From the moment the lights came up and 'Land of Make Believe' started playing, I was full of adrenaline and dancing my socks off. I would not say that I made the best Prince Charming in the world, but I gave it my best shot. Most of the time I stayed at home between shows, but we were in Cornwall two nights a week and Q'dos had arranged for an overnight stay in a pub. This was supposedly haunted, and I would get so scared at bedtime that I kept the light on, much to the annoyance of the girl I was sharing a room with. I'd generally drink so much on those nights that I'd knock myself out, and then have to pull myself together for the two shows the next day. We looked after each other as a cast, helped each other improve and got hyped up together before performances.

The other two girls in the show were a size or two smaller than me in clothes. I'd become very self conscious of my weight at the time. I ate and drank whatever I liked, but it dawned on me that a little more self-control was required. The 'problem' was that I was still a very fussy vegetarian with an affinity for bread and sugar. Looking back, it was not a great cause for concern. As a UK size 8-10, it was only my association with the dance world that made me feel so insecure. My height didn't help matters either. This is the first instance I really recall comparing myself to others and wanting to lose weight. My Mum encouraged this. As much as she would tell me I was beautiful, she'd also be quick to point out if I was eating too much junk food or if I'd put on a couple of pounds. She told me this out of love, but it battered my already low confidence and allowed my negative self-talk to kick in.

"You're fat, you're not good enough, you're not going to get work looking like this," I told myself.

I decided to enrol on an Open University degree, just in case I didn't make it in show business. I chose Psychology and Philosophy, as these were the subjects I'd most enjoyed at school. I thought that through the winter period, when demand was low, I'd be able to spend time studying.

Luckily, I did still have a role to look forward to in Scarborough that winter. At an entertainments host seminar, I'd been lucky enough to meet Daniel Defoe, who worked in The Shearings Hotel there. I called him to ask if he knew of anyone with a spare room I could rent for the duration of the pantomime run. He soon came back to me with a better offer: he and his partner, Chris, offered me a room at their home. I was over the moon, as Daniel was a lot of fun and, although I'd never met Chris,

I knew he was a fabulous female-impersonator cabaret-act. I was looking forward to staying with them and seeing them perform.

When the time came, I started my Nissan Micra and, with my parents waving me off, promptly banged into the gate post. Not the best start. While Dad patched up the car, Mum made me a cup of tea and dried my tears. Then it was time for take two and I drove off to my first winter pantomime season.

The Spa Theatre sits right on Scarborough seafront and seats 600 people. We had quite a lot of evening sell-out shows, performed matinees, and even held morning performances for school children. It was a full-on schedule. I was the Good Fairy, who mainly answered back to the Wicked Queen to try and persuade her to leave Snow White and her friends alone. The part gave me a five-minute magic solo in the show, in which amongst other visual, colourful trickery, I made a magical heart appear in the forest. This I gave to the woodcutter, so that he could pretend to the Wicked Queen that he had cut out Snow White's heart. I loved performing the magic and adored the reaction it got, especially from the children who would gasp in delight. The proper stage lights and music from the band added to a really atmospheric performance.

It was very chilly backstage, and I got quite run down with colds during the season. Chris and Daniel introduced me to whiskey and brandy at this point, and after returning home, I'd have a hot toddy with them or just a shot before bed. I also started keeping a bottle of Jagermeister backstage, telling the other cast members that it was an essential herbal liquor that helped my voice when it was croaky. In all honesty, this was true, and I'd never have more than a tiny sip before performing anyway.

There were some cast nights out to various restaurants, pubs and the casino. The cast and crew got on like a house on fire, which made Scarborough a fun place to be, despite the cold. My parents visited to see the show and to celebrate my birthday for a few days around New Year's Eve. They stayed in the Shearings hotel, and I was booked to sing there on New Year's Eve too, which was a great night. I was very sad to leave Scarborough, especially my new friends Chris and Daniel who had looked after me so well.

Upon my return, I recommenced my magical training with Richard Leigh. Over the winter he had designed a self-levitation illusion for me, as well as some other, smaller illusions that I could use in my show. We worked really hard so that I'd be able to perform through the summer season, and when it was all put together, my 45 minute speciality act ran as follows:

- Colourful, clever magic with silks and flowers, punctuated with glitter.
- Some audience interaction and the paper hat trick.
- Another pretty magic routine with colour changing CDs.
- Dolly Parton dress-up / vocal routine. This included breasts made out of balloons, which I then magically pushed a needle through.
- Comedy routine, in which I selected a man from the audience to choose a card. I then performed a mini-illusion putting a sword 'through his neck'.

Then, I stole his underpants (prop ones) and the card he had chosen happened to be inside them.
- Grand finale, starting with a dance with two long silks and ending with the self-levitation illusion.

I performed this routine solidly at hotels and holiday centres around the South West for three years. It was a big show to set up and some of the venues were awkward to carry everything in to, so I trained up two roadies. Either my little brother Daniel or my friend's son Kyle would come with me on the journeys, which gave me some company and lightened the load of the bulkier items. Then we'd spend around an hour setting up the show, after which I'd do my stage makeup and get changed before performing. After the show we'd tidy everything away so it was ready to go again next time. With all the travelling, setting up and breaking down, it could take up to seven hours out of our day to deliver a 45-minute show. On top of this, there was constant ironing of silks and the preparing and mending of props that I had to do at home. It was lovely spending the time with Daniel though: it reminded me of the days when Mum and I would perform shows together, then listen to music and eat junk food on the way home. Daniel loved magic and wanted to watch Derren Brown and Jeff Mcbride when they were touring near us, which meant we spent that extra time together too. He even taught himself some complex card flourishes!

Through the main six weeks of the 2008 summer season I was again offered work with Q'dos, this time another pirate show and 'Beauty and the Beast', in which I played Fairy and added in some magical effects. The tour ran at the Haven Centres in Somerset, Devon and

Weymouth. I was cast with the couple I had worked with the year before, who were now performing illusions having also worked with Richard Leigh. This helped them present a fabulous transformation effect for the 'Beast to Prince' scene. I'd also recommended a lady I worked with in the Scarborough pantomime to join the cast, and following a successful audition, she became 'Belle'. She stayed with me for most of the summer, having come from Yorkshire. The comedy impressionist I'd worked with in my first season for Q'dos, and a fabulous dancer who'd performed in many West End shows, completed our cast. We would finish our evening performances at around 8pm, meaning that on some nights I had time to run to a local hotel and perform my magical speciality act too. It was another busy, but fun summer.

I spent the winter season performing in the local hotels back in Torbay, then, with a little money saved from three years of touring and living in my parent's granny flat, started looking for a house. I consulted with my parents who put me in touch with a financial advisor and came to view some places with me. I fell in love with a one-bedroom coach house with a huge garage underneath, which would be perfect for storing my props and costumes. It was a new build, so I was able to choose my own decor and colours, and I loved the thought of being in a place that I could put my own stamp on. Mum helped me haggle over the price and my mortgage went through, which allowed me to move in in February 2009. Friends helped me get settled, and I even threw a couple of little gatherings. Q'dos had been instrumental in getting me my own house, and I felt so grateful.

Everything felt like it was going my way at the start of 2009. Little did I know what the next year would bring.

Chapter 7 – A Family Affair

Pain.

Despair.

Loss.

Guilt.

Hopelessness.

These were just some of the feelings that flooded me when my Bobe died.

We knew it was coming. Bobe had bravely battled Parkinson's Disease for 16 years and, although I had no clue about the subtle beginnings of her illness, it became increasingly pronounced in her final few years. When I was 14, my grandparents moved out of the big house that held so many memories for them, and moved into a bungalow because of Bobe's mobility issues. My parents and I then moved into their house. Bobe had always been so lively, fun and motivated, but this cruel disease wore her down. It made her jittery and it slurred her speech. More than anything, it just wasn't fair: of all the people in the world to be afflicted with such a dreadful illness, the best person in mine was being taken by this.

I found it hard to watch what it did to her. Although I still visited my grandparents a lot, I was also a typical 23-year-old - out with friends, working, drinking, pretending it wasn't happening and that the inevitable wasn't coming. Some days were better than others, so I would always hope to catch her on good form when I visited and that she could still make conversation and sing with me.

I'd been offered jobs abroad, both to dance and perform with my magic, but I had never taken any long contracts. I hadn't wanted to be away from Bobe and Wizzo, just in case anything happened to them. Then in December 2009, I was in pantomime in Lincolnshire, playing the part of the magical Genie in 'Aladdin'. When I left to perform in the show, Wizzo was fit and healthy and Bobe was stable. However I got a call from Mum after an evening performance on 15th December and it floored me completely.

"We've had to put Wizzo to sleep," her shaky voice came down the line.

"What do you mean? No..."

Mum told me that our sweet little dog had been poorly in the night, whining and drinking a lot. They took her to the vets who diagnosed her with kidney and liver failure. The vet had given her some medication, then instructed Mum and Dad to see how she was in the morning and make a decision. The damage was irreversible. The medication only held off the suffering for a few hours, after which she was crying in pain again. Mum and Dad went back to the vet and then Wizzo was gone.

I remember crumbling into a heap in the middle of the street. One of the cast members from the show came and picked me up, and I just leant into him and wept. We had no shows the next day, Sunday, so he offered to drive me to my paternal grandparents' house in Sheffield, so at least I could be with family. Grandad met us halfway there on the motorway, cuddled me and spoke soothingly to me on the way home. Grandma made me some food when we arrived back, but I didn't feel like eating and I didn't sleep much that night either. I couldn't understand why Mum hadn't waited for me to see Wizzo one last time.

I called her back the next day and asked the question.

"Ami, it was time sensitive. She was in a lot of pain. The vet could have given me more medication to ease that for another few hours, but you'd have let everyone down by missing a show. It would also have been a 12 hour round trip for you to get here and back. I thought about it, discussed it with your Dad, but I've done this for you."

I didn't understand or agree for a long time. To me, Wizzo was more important than any show, job or indeed anything. Now she was gone and I hadn't been able to say goodbye. I'd always said I'd never work abroad in case this happened, but a pantomime in Lincolnshire had kept me away just the same.

I got home from Lincolnshire at the start of January 2010. I'd forgiven my parents by this time, although I was still distraught at the circumstances. Luckily, Bobe was OK for now, but over the next few weeks she deteriorated, unable to eat or drink properly as her swallow reflex and digestive muscles slowed down.

The night before she fell into a coma, Mum called me to say I should go over to my grandparents' house to see her. I was out with friends at a pub quiz at the time, so I promised to visit the next day.

However, when the next day came, she was already sound asleep. I've always wished I'd listened to my Mum on that occasion. Mum, Grandad, my Auntie Linda, Great Aunt Sybil, Uncle David and I held a five day bedside vigil with her. At night, Grandad slept in their spare room with David, whilst Mum, Linda, and I made camp on the floor in the lounge. The tiny, 84-year-old Sybil had the luxury of the sofa to sleep on. During this time, I talked to Bobe and held her hand. Sometimes she squeezed mine back or made a mumbling sound. The carers said she wasn't aware of what was going on, but I believe she felt my presence.

On 2nd February 2010, Mum was hosting a big showcase event in Cornwall. She had recently taken over a new agency down there, and while she didn't want to leave the house to attend the event, Grandad insisted.

"The show must go on," he said simply.

Eventually he persuaded Mum that Bobe would have wanted it to be that way, and in reality Mum had to show her face with all the new clients she'd invited. I accompanied her to give her strength and lighten the load, because at the time I was helping to run the Cornwall office with her. Something inside me told me that it was a good idea to go.

We had a very successful evening in Truro and the show was fantastic.

Afterwards, the crew, who were aware of our situation, said they'd tidy up so that we could get back.

We said our goodbyes to the clients and left. Mum called David when we got into the car and put the phone on loudspeaker.

"She's gone," he said.

Mum sobbed. She felt we shouldn't have left the house that night, but it was at this point that I realised why I had felt so strongly about going. I loved my Bobe, and she would never have wanted me to see her lifeless. She'd passed away when I left the house to protect me. I told Mum through my tears and said I was sorry. She understood, of course.

We went back to the house. Mum wanted to see her mother that night, so she went into the room and I heard her crying. Then we slept on the floor of my grandparents' house for one last night.

Bobe's funeral was an incredibly difficult day. I don't actually remember much of it, other than that the church was absolutely full to the brim with people. I knew there would be a lot of people there, and I wasn't really up to talking, so the day before I went to see my hairdresser and had her dye my hair. It had been light blonde for years, but I chose a dark brown colour so I wouldn't be as conspicuous. Some of my friends came along to the funeral for moral support, including my friend James, who I had known since primary school and who I clung to at the wake. Any time I tried to speak I just cried, so it was better that I spent time with people who wouldn't ask too many questions and just let me be.

Grieving is such a personal process. I found it unhelpful when people would tell me not to cry or to be strong. Sometimes I think that people say these things because they don't know how to deal with the emotions they are feeling themselves. I did not need to be strong, I needed to cry, to grieve and to heal. I felt lucky to be able to escape to a couple of good friends' houses, who understood that I needed some space from my family, who I was trying to be strong for, and cry. We would just sit and watch TV, not speaking, with them making sure I ate occasionally. Sometimes all you need is silent company. When words can't help or heal, you have to try and come to terms with things rather than ignoring them and busying yourself.

Bobe was an amazingly positive influence on my life for which I am eternally grateful. Though she is gone, I always feel that there is a part of her deep in my heart.

Mum took over Trevor George Entertainments from my grandparents when I was 12-years-old. At first she continued to work as an illusionist in the evenings, but cut down her schedule to accommodate the extra work. She became extremely successful and grew the agency so much that in 1999 she had to stop working in the evenings altogether and take on two extra members of staff.

The agency still ran from our house at that time, so I'd come home from school, hear the phones ringing and make cups of tea for everyone if I was in the right sort of mood. Mum was always very busy, so I'd go and do my homework, go to my dance classes or chill out with Dad. I'd been used to having the agency in my grandparents' house, so it wasn't too different.

By the time I was working in the agency, after I came home from London in 2004, it was located in new premises, and she now employed four members of staff. Mum worked from 8 a.m. to 10 p.m. some days, as she liked to get to work early to have a quiet, productive start before anyone else arrived. She was then on call most evenings and at weekends in case an acts' car broke down on the way to work or they had a problem. When I started working with her, I took a little of the pressure off by being on call myself a couple of nights a week.

Whenever I worked for Q'dos or in pantomime, I was away for long periods. However when I came back, I'd often go to work in the office to help out as there was always a job to be done.

In 2009, Mum heard that Kernow Entertainments in Cornwall was being sold and decided that since it was so close to us, she would take it over. I was still performing a few nights a week, but as this was mainly in Devon and Cornwall anyway, Mum asked if I would like to help her with the merging of the agencies. I jumped at the chance and started visiting clients in Cornwall with her to introduce ourselves and find out their requirements. I started working a couple of days a week in the office in Falmouth alongside the staff who were already employed there. It was a quiet office compared to the one in Torquay, so I busied myself by looking into new venues and finding additional business. I also started sourcing talent in the area and organised an audition so we could find some acts. The main difference between the offices was the type of gigs we were booking: in Cornwall there was more demand for wedding acts and event entertainment, so I learnt about that side of the industry and attended some wedding fairs.

After completing the pantomime run in Lincolnshire that winter, I returned to the Falmouth office for three days a week. I would sing in the local hotels in the evenings or rest at the guest house I stayed in. There, I made friends with the owners and their beautiful greyhound.

The evening of Bobe's passing had been the first big showcase event we held down there, the perfect chance for clients to see our most recommended artistes, so it had been an important night. It had been successful too: as a result of the evening, we had many bookings and the office was very busy. Alongside working in the Falmouth office I completed my NVQ in Customer Services and arranged for other members of staff to complete theirs too. I felt it was important that we had the chance to develop and gain some rewards.

As much as I'd been enjoying working in the agency and performing my shows, the deaths of two family members in the space of two months had hit me hard. I didn't have the same drive or interest that I'd had before. I think we all assumed that at some point I'd get back to being my 'normal' self, but I didn't. I went through the motions, got my work done and went out partying and drinking to forget.

Mum, Grandad and I visited Paris in May 2010. He had visited this romantic city with Bobe on a couple of occasions, and loved showing us around all the highlights. We had a lot of fun together, and it was exactly what we'd needed after a difficult few months. We visited the Lido and the Moulin Rouge to watch the incredible cabaret shows, climbed the Eiffel Tower, and marvelled at Notre Dame, the Louvre and Montmartre. The only thing that did not impress me was the lack of vegetarian options, or understanding of them. Whenever

I said "no meat", I was offered fish, so I ended up on a diet of mainly lettuce and croissants that week.

In July, Mum asked if I'd be able to go and help out with the Q'dos tour that was currently in Wales, as the magician in the show had fallen sick. I'd originally turned down the tour as I wanted to be able to enjoy my new house and persevere with my degree, but I thought that a couple of weeks away could be helpful for me. I was right. I loved Tenby and New Quay, and while I spent the evenings performing, my days were filled with adventure on the beaches and in the quaint little Welsh towns. I breathed in the air, relaxed and felt better than I had done in months.

Upon my return, I decided that I would do something for me and for Bobe. My grandparents had always loved exploring different countries, and when I was little, they would often go away and come back with stories and photographs of their adventures.

"You must travel Ami," I remembered Bobe saying.

Grandad was the Chairman of the local branch of the Parkinson's Disease Society at that time, an organisation that had been so helpful to my family throughout the last few years of Bobe's life. I decided that I would trek 100km in the Sahara Desert as a tribute to her, as well as to raise money for the charity. The expedition was to be in October 2011, so I had some time to gather funds and do the necessary training.

I decided that now was also the time to find a new animal companion. I'd lived with dogs all of my life and spending six months without one had been lonely and sad. They gave me more comfort than anyone I knew. My parents were really against the idea, because I'd been touring and working a lot and they didn't want to be left looking after a puppy all the time. However, because I was working nearer to home and had friends who could help me out, I started researching my options.

I was at the hairdressers one day, discussing the issue, when I got a tip, "The lady who works in the opticians next door has the most gorgeous dogs. You must see them!"

As she waited for my colour to dry, the hairdresser popped next door and came back with a smiling lady who was waving her phone, ready to show me several photographs of her long haired dachshunds. Ruby and Oscar were certainly gorgeous dogs, but I had my questions, mostly about if they could even run on such short legs. I was assured by Sue, the owner, that the dogs were in proportion and could certainly run when they wanted to.

We exchanged numbers, and Sue told me I'd be welcome to meet her dachshunds whenever I wanted to. I called her soon after and arranged a walk. She had been right: what these curious dogs lacked in size, they more than made up for in character and spirit. We had a lovely walk, with Oscar running around chasing a ball the entire time. Sue said she would pass my number on to the breeder and assured me that if I was offered a puppy, she would be happy to help with some dog sitting duties in the evenings if I was working. I went home, quietly optimistic.

A few days later, I received a call from a well-spoken lady named Melissa. She quizzed me on where I lived, what I could offer a dachshund puppy and if I'd had dogs before. Having considered my responses, she told me she'd be in touch in the future. I decided to keep looking in the meantime, as I didn't want to put all my eggs in one basket. Luckily though, Melissa called again two days later to say that she had two puppies and asked if I would like to see them. She'd had to check out my address and references before considering accepting me as a suitable owner. I told Mum who, although reluctant at first, was quite excited about the idea and wanted to come with me to meet the puppies.

The dogs were just two weeks old when we were invited to meet them for the first time, with their mother, in a jewellery shop in Babbacombe. One was black and tan, the other a bright golden colour, or "shaded red" as Melissa described it. They hadn't yet opened their eyes and stayed close to their mother in their crate. We were able to pick them up for cuddles though; I'd never held such a tiny dog!

"Mum, we will have to take them both, I can't pick one!"

"You'll have to," Melissa answered, "one has been reserved by the owners of the shop opposite me. You get to pick which is yours though."

How could I choose between them? I asked the mother of the litter for her advice, and slowly but definitely she nosed the golden puppy.

"She's ours!" I said excitedly, giving her a final cuddle before we left the shop so they could suckle and snooze.

I told Melissa on my next visit, "Her name is Priscilla, Queen of the Dachshunds!" Ever since, we've called her Cilla for short.

I visited Cilla frequently so we could bond before I took her home. Mum sometimes came along too, and offered to help when she came home. Our little dog had wrapped us both around her tiny paw. She came home in September at nine weeks old, just after I'd finished a busy summer season of shows. I had two weeks off to help her settle in at home, and we spent that time playing and snoozing. Cilla was toilet trained from the beginning, having lived with Melissa's pack of seven in her home. She slept through the night from the word go, as if she knew she had found her home with me straight away. I'd purchased a bag for Cilla so I could take her out with me before her injections and introduce her to friends. We also had many visitors which meant that she was extremely well socialised from the beginning.

When I went back to doing some shows, Sue, Melissa and Mum all chipped in to puppy-sit. When I worked in the agency in the daytime, I took her with me and she'd alternate between napping in a basket under my desk, finding paper to rip up and identifying shoes to chew. She made everyone smile.

I was enjoying motherhood and feeling settled in my new home. Yet I wasn't getting the same buzz from my shows in the way that I had done previously. I enjoyed performing in a theatre, where people had paid to see the show and thus sat and appreciated it, but this work was not available all year round. The holiday centre work was not as fulfilling. I practised hard to refine my solo cabaret act, but in the end I often felt like a babysitter for the kids of parents who just sat drinking and chatting throughout my performance.

I talked things through with Mum and decided to take a break for a couple of months at the start of the New Year, as soon as I had finished all my Christmas shows. January is always a quiet month for entertainment, as a lot of the hotels in Torbay are closed.

I felt low and as if I wasn't reaching my full potential, but knew that with a month of reflection to consider the options, I could decide which path I wanted to choose next.

Chapter 8 – The Next Stage

During my month off I had time to relax and listen to what my body was telling me. I played with Cilla and took her for walks and to training classes. I also did some hiking in preparation for my upcoming desert trek, which gave me time to think. I did not miss doing my act, so I looked at alternative employment instead. In fact in hindsight, I realised how nervous and anxious I had become waiting in the wings to see what sort of audience would be in the venues each night. Would they pay attention and have some fun, or groan when they heard it was a 'magic act' and ignore most of my show?

I asked myself a very simple question: "What do I love?" The answers were pretty simple.

I still loved dancing. I couldn't imagine a life without dance. I looked through 'The Stage' newspaper to see if any of the dance jobs interested me. It would be difficult for me to go away for a contract now I had committed to Cilla. Then, something caught my eye - an advert to train as a street dance teacher. I had always preferred tap and commercial dance over ballet, and I thought back to how much I'd loved attending Miss Marisa's classes as a child. I looked up the website and found that the business offering the course had been going for a while, with franchises of dance schools around the UK. The snippets of class footage looked like fun, and at the time, no one was particularly specializing in teaching street dance in Torbay. I thought this might be something I could bring to the studios in the area, so I phoned the number and spoke with a lady named Hayley to discuss the ins and outs of the course. She checked that I had the relevant dance qualifications, and I decided that I had nothing to lose by signing-up. The course would be a week-long, intensive session, taking place in the capital in February. I had just one month to wait, so I arranged some accommodation in London and got in touch with some local studios to assess the market. Marisa told me that she already had someone teaching street dance, but would be interested in me running a musical theatre course instead. She asked if I would meet with her to discuss this, which I did. The Riviera Centre would be able to rent their studio space to me after school on Wednesday afternoons, while Winners studio could host me on a Monday evening and Aztec studio could offer me a Friday evening slot. I booked myself in to start at the venues in March. The studios designed some wonderful promotional material for me, which meant I could get the word out in advance. I contacted my local paper to do a piece on me too. Marisa would be promoting my course in-house to her current students, but said I could also advertise on my website and Facebook page. With that, 'So Street', my dance-teaching business, was born.

My other love was animals. I'd been a vegetarian for over ten years at this point, and I loved being with Cilla. Whenever I walked past a dog I would stop to admire and coo at it. I had also enjoyed my time in my early teens with Jo, Debbie and the horses. When I was a little girl, I thought that being a vet would be amazing, and envisaged myself helping animals all day. However, as I grew up and understood the mortality aspect, I went off this idea.

I was looking through the Job Centre website one day, when an advert caught my eye. *'Visitor Liaison Officer required for Equine Charity'*. I applied straight away for their part-time position, as the thought of working with horses really appealed to me. I didn't have much experience, but I was good with people generally and was willing to learn. I was offered an interview at the Mare and Foal Sanctuary in early February, and on the day arrived at the visitor centre in plenty of time to be sure of making a good impression.

Pulling up in the car park, I was greeted with the familiar scent of horses and the outdoors. I saw the acres of land and felt the peace of the place; I loved it already. I breathed in and prayed that the interview would go well.

At the reception, a smiling lady called Teresa introduced herself as the centre manager and signed me in. She told me that I would be interviewed by herself and one of the directors, Simon. We went through to the office and I was offered a cup of tea. During the interview, she asked me if I would mind sitting at a desk and doing a typing task, as some of the job would entail writing up programmes and meeting minutes. I was happy to do so, as my experience both in the agency and temping meant that I was able to touch type with some confidence. I was asked to copy a short paragraph about a hermaphrodite horse called Kavaner, from which they would be able to check my timing and accuracy. Afterwards, they asked if I had any questions.

"Is Kavaner real?" I asked.

"Yes," Teresa smiled, "I'll introduce you to him shortly. We just have a few interview questions for you first."

She and Simon asked me some questions relating to my work history and aspirations. I remember smiling a lot to try and win them over, and compensate for my lack of experience.

Once the interview was over, we walked out to the main yard so I could meet the horses and ponies. Teresa started telling me about each one; how they'd come to be at the Sanctuary, what their character traits were and where they currently were with regards to training. I met the famous Kavaner, a gorgeous, gentle Shire horse who nuzzled Teresa's head. Simon asked if I would be able to give a short demo tour as part of my interview. He said he understood that I didn't know any facts about the horses per se, but wanted to hear me present as I would to visitors. I was in my element doing this, as it was just like acting on stage. Simon and Teresa both gave me great feedback on the spot, saying how impressed they were that I'd remembered some of the details mentioned to me earlier and how confidently I came across. I loved the horses, had grown fond of Teresa and was desperate to get the job there.

I got a call from Teresa the next day. I had popped into Mum's office at the time, so I went into the kitchen area for some privacy. Mum held up crossed fingers as I closed the door.

"Hi Ami, we really enjoyed meeting you and you interviewed really well yesterday. Unfortunately, we are unable to offer you the job at this time, as someone with more experience also applied and has accepted the offer."

"That's OK. Thank you so much for your time. I loved coming to the Sanctuary and would love to know more about volunteering with you anyway," I told her. She promised to email me a volunteer application form and hung up.

I went into Mum's office with tears in my eyes, "I didn't get it."

"Ami, they will call you back. I have a feeling about this," she said with determination, then put her arms around me to comfort me.

Sure enough, two days later, Teresa was back on the phone to tell me that the lady she had offered the job to originally had turned it down. Apparently she wasn't keen on driving down the country lanes. Teresa continued to tell me that, providing I hadn't found anything yet, I would be their next choice.

I was delighted and accepted on the spot. We set a date for the beginning of March, as I still had my street dance teaching course to attend, for me to start working at the Coombe Park Visitor Centre three days per week. I felt the happiest I had in ages. Outdoor life with horses would suit me down to the ground and would be a million miles away from show business. I gave Mum the good news.

"I told you so," she said, proudly.

The next week I went off to London for five full days of dance. We had been asked to prepare some choreography ready for the start of the course, which we would then learn how to break down and teach using NLP (neuro linguistic programming) methods. There were ten of us attending for the week, all at different stages and abilities in our dance careers. I felt really nervous starting on the first day, but I needn't have worried. Everyone was lovely, friendly and so enthusiastic about dance. We all supported and cheered each other as we each took turns in leading 'classes' and giving constructive feedback. We learnt as much from each other as we did from the trainers. I just hoped that upon returning to Torquay, I'd be able to keep the excitement and energy just as high for my students.

I started my career in dance teaching at Marisa's studio, teaching musical theatre classes. I remembered some of the vocal exercises I used to do during my course in Nottingham, and had brought some poems for them to read aloud. I had also choreographed a routine to 'Consider Yourself' from 'Oliver'. Marisa oversaw my first couple of classes, then left me to my own devices once she felt assured that I was capable. She asked if I'd like to help the children through some IDTA (International Dance Teachers' Association) exams, for which they would need to perform some specific exercises and a group piece that I had helped develop for an external examiner. Marisa gave me the syllabus to teach, and the children were ready for exams just before Christmas that year. All of them passed with merit or above, and I was extremely proud of them and myself.

At Aztec, Winners and the Riviera Centre, the children's street dance classes were quiet. As studios that normally hosted adult fitness classes, I felt like I may have chosen the wrong venues for them. However, my adult classes at Aztec and Winners were busy and I loved teaching them. Children can sometimes have a 'can't do that' attitude, whereas the adults were always happy to give things a good go and have a laugh with it.

I enjoyed choosing music for the classes each week – modern and old school R'n'B, hip hop and pop. I taught at Aztec on a Friday night and called it the 'warm-up to the weekend'. Some weeks, friends would come along to join in with the class, then we'd go back to my house to get ready to go out clubbing. My classes at Winners were on a Monday night, and my brother Daniel often attended with his friends. It became a mainly male-dominated dance class.

My employment at The Mare and Foal Sanctuary was just as perfect as I'd imagined. I got on really well with Teresa and my other Visitor Liaison colleague, Sarah. The job involved promoting the Sanctuary, leading visitor tours, running events and selling merchandise. As it was a cause I was passionate about, I was able to talk at length about the horses once I'd got to know them, and visitors would often leave good-sized donations. In my lunch breaks, I'd go down to the yard to spend time with the ponies and groom them or chat to them and find out more about their personalities. I obviously had my favourites, but generally just being around horses calmed me down and made me smile. All the stress from my show business career was starting to dissipate.

At the end of March 2011, I attended a two day fitness event in London that I'd seen advertised when I'd been there for my teacher training. I thought I might glean some inspiration or pick up some ideas for my current classes; if nothing else, I would have a fun couple of days doing back-to-back dance and fitness classes. I arrived at the huge exhibition centre and grabbed a programme. There was so much going on, so I decided to just wander around the halls first to get my bearings and see if anything jumped out at me. It did. Tucked away in a small area was a beautiful, tiny Indian girl. She was dancing, smiling and encouraging people to join in. I stopped to watch her for a moment, and she came over to introduce herself to me.

"Hi, I'm Shalini. I'm about to start a taster 'Just Jhoom!' Bollywood dance fitness class. Would you like to join in?" It sounded fun, and I'd instantly warmed to Shalini, so I agreed.

Just Jhoom! was so different. It got my heart rate up with its aerobic-style movements, and the traditional Indian hand and arm motions were so feminine and pretty. The best thing about it was the music though – so fun and catchy! Shalini was a great presenter and made us all laugh with her cheeky comments and personality. After the class, she came to talk to me again, asking me about my dance experience and what I was currently teaching.

"I'm running a Just Jhoom! teaching course in July. You should sign up. If you use the code from this show and sign up in the next couple of weeks, I'll even give you a discount."

There were definitely no Bollywood classes running in Torbay. Bellydance, yes, which is very different, but nothing like this. The fitness element meant the adult studios I was teaching in would possibly take an interest too. I took away the information so I could talk to Mum about it when I got home, then spent the rest of my time at the exhibition enjoying other fitness classes, sports massages and healthy food. Nothing appealed to me like Just Jhoom! had though.

Mum, who was so supportive of me at this time, also thought Just Jhoom! was a great idea and encouraged me to enrol on the course.

Similar to my street dancing classes, I promoted the idea to the studios before my training was complete, which enabled me to start teaching as soon as my training was done. Aztec were happy for me to stop the children's street class and replace it with the Just Jhoom! class, alongside a second Wednesday morning class there. I also had to do some free Just Jhoom! classes and video them as part of my qualification, so they agreed to let me do that over the summer. Winners let me change my children's class to Just Jhoom! too, but The Riviera Centre had no availability and my children's classes hadn't picked up, so I gave notice there. Marisa was extremely excited about having a new class to offer to the older children and their parents.

The main worry I had in my life now was financial. I had taken a huge pay cut going from shows to working part-time for a charity with a dance business I was still building. I had some savings in the bank and promised myself I would put my mental health before my finances, but with a mortgage and bills to pay, I knew I needed to find a way to increase my income before things became difficult. Luckily, the answers came to me in good time. Marisa asked me if I'd like to take on some extra musical theatre classes at a studio in Newton Abbot, where the owner was keen for the students to do some IDTA exams. I also had a call from a lady in Totnes, who had seen my website and wanted to take on a street dance teacher for four classes a week at her new studio. Following meetings with both studio owners, and after persuading the one in Totnes that Bollywood would also be a great addition to the studio, I started work in September 2011.

The next course I decided to take was Cheerobics – a blend of Cheerleading and aerobics. I was able to complete this course online with the trainer, Jessica, then submit videos for feedback in the same way that I had for Just Jhoom! Jessica was very encouraging, and when I introduced the class to my current clients, they loved waving around their pom poms and found it a good way to tone up. I waved goodbye to some of the classes that weren't doing as well and replaced them with Cheerobics in March 2012.

I had an idea at this time about offering dance parties for children's birthdays. While I had been performing magic, I had sometimes done children's parties and still got an occasional enquiry, so I thought why not offer them a different style of party instead? I put together some promotional materials for children's street dance, Disney dance, cheer dance and Bollywood dance parties and added this to my website. Enquiries started rolling in. I was also approached by some agencies who coordinated hen parties, asking if I could provide dance lessons to hens in the Torbay area, so I added this to my repertoire as well. I was happy to customise the theme to whatever the hens wanted – Dirty Dancing style, Michael Jackson, 80s, Grease, to name a few. Hen parties soon became my favourite type of engagement, as they were a great laugh and I was able to be really creative with them.

I had a lot of energy, which I needed. I was working 3 days a week at the Mare and Foal Sanctuary, which often involved physical tasks when getting ready for events, and I was teaching 15 classes per week. I had regular sports massages and chiropractic treatment to help my muscles and joints, which were often tight and sore. I have hyper mobility, a condition that causes me to over-stretch, meaning that wear and tear occurs at a higher rate. Some days, I was in a lot of discomfort: trapped nerves always caused the worst pain. I loved what I was doing though.

Unfortunately, it can seem that when your life is going really well, something comes along to trip you up. I was at home with my friends Nem (short for Naomi) and Steph, who I went to school with, one evening. We'd had an evening of gossip, pizza and homemade cocktails, put the world to rights and laughed a lot. Cilla was sat on the sofa relaxing in our company. Suddenly, she went rigid and wide eyed, her limbs started jerking. I picked her up,

"Cilla?" I said desperately and stroked her, looking into her eyes, "Cilla? I need to phone the vet. Is she dying?"

"I'm not sure what's happening," Nem grabbed my phone and found the vet's number. She put it on loudspeaker so I could talk while holding Cilla. It took what felt like a lifetime to get through to the vet, whose phone was diverted as it was already after hours. Cilla stopped shaking, then wet herself. Nem went to find some kitchen towels to clean up the mess.

"Hi, there's something seriously wrong with Cilla," I described the symptoms to the vet, who asked me a few questions, then told me that the event sounded like a seizure. I was instructed to bring her in the next day.

"Are you sure it'll wait until then?" I asked. "She's never done this before, I'm really worried."

The vet reassured me, "Yes, most dogs will only have one. Now she's gone back to normal there's nothing we can do now that we couldn't do tomorrow. If she has another one, phone me straight back, but otherwise we'll see you then."

I didn't sleep a wink all night. I slept on the floor with Cilla, worried in case she started seizing again.

The next morning, Mum accompanied me to the vet, who gave Cilla a thorough examination and told me she seemed fine, but was still cautious.

"We'll take some blood tests just in case there's anything underlying. It could be a one-off, but the chances are if she has another one, it's idiopathic epilepsy."

She gave me some liquid diazepam to administer rectally to Cilla, in case she had another seizure that lasted for over five minutes, and sent us on our way. I organised for someone to be with Cilla constantly over the next couple of weeks to monitor her at all times, because I still had to work, but nothing happened and she seemed more or less okay. The blood tests all came back normal.

Four months later, Cilla had another seizure at home. I used the rectal diazepam, which helped her relax and come out of it, but this time she urinated, defecated and was violently sick. I took her back to the vet the next morning. She told me that Cilla had lost a lot of fluid and would need to stay in on a drip overnight. Then she confirmed her diagnosis of idiopathic epilepsy.

The seizures cropped up every few months. I lived on edge, wondering how best to live with this disease that had invaded our lives. Luckily, I had so much support from Mum, Sue, Melissa, Nem and several other friends, who all offered to help care for Cilla when I was working and support me when things seemed tough. Cilla was so happy between seizures and I was determined to give her the best life possible.

In January 2013 I decided to interview for a new position at the Mare and Foal Sanctuary. I loved the Visitor Liaison work and my time with the ponies, but I also felt that I wanted to learn some new things, so was pleased that an opportunity had presented itself. I went to the main office at Honeysuckle Farm to be interviewed by Jerry, the Human Resources manager, for an HR and Health and Safety Assistant position. I was told a week later that I had been successful. I would now be working four days a week at Honeysuckle Farm, the organisation's main equine rehabilitation site that was closed to the public. Although I wasn't working with the horses in my new role, I made it my mission to get to know them in my lunch breaks and find out as much as I could about the rehabilitation process. I spoke to Syra, the equine director, about volunteering on the yard. She was happy for me to do so, so I started off doing an hour or two here and there on my days off, after which she asked if I'd like to do some extra paid shifts on the yard at the weekends. If I wasn't involved in dance teaching or performing, I always said yes. My favourite pony at Coombe Park had been a little spotted fellow called

Sumo. He was rescued a couple of years before I joined the Sanctuary team and had been on loan as a companion pony, but he came back during the first Summer I spent there. He was very loving and had a fun character, so I was sad to leave him behind when I moved. Unfortunately, Sumo had a condition called Uveitis, which impaired his vision and caused ulcers in his eyes. This meant that he needed to be moved from the visitor centre to Honeysuckle Farm, which allowed him to have more targeted treatment and care. I was happy to have him back with me and to be able to see him on my lunch breaks each day.

I enjoyed my new role, learning about contracts, employment law, risk assessments and procedures. It might not sound fun, but when the topic revolves around horses and farm equipment, it's actually very interesting. Jerry, who had been in human resources for a number of years, was a great teacher.

The other amazing part of working at Honeysuckle Farm was that I could bring Cilla into the office on days when no one else could look after her. This made a massive difference to me, as I worried about leaving her on her own now due to her seizures. I tried not to overdo it and could generally find someone else to look after her, but knowing I had this as a backup saved me a lot of stress. I stayed at Honeysuckle Farm in the same role, besides a small break, until October 2017. I always enjoyed the variety of working in an equine welfare sanctuary and loved the people and horses I shared this time with. I felt at home, and that I had really landed on my feet.

Chapter 9 – African Adventures

I breathed in the hot, sweet, arid air and exhaled a smile. I felt relaxed and at ease.

"What will we see today?" I asked Mohammed,

"Ami, just let it happen. Enjoy the day. You don't need to know everything."

This was good, but disconcerting advice for someone who was used to planning their days meticulously. I fell in step beside him though, smiling, breathing and enjoying the vastness of the Sahara. It is a powerful place; everything is the same, but different. Sand everywhere, dunes, occasional trees and clear night skies full of stars.

We travelled with the Bedouin and each day, they'd get up early to move our tents to the next overnight stopping point. Mohammed led the trek, and when we hit points of interest, such as the Sahara's largest sand dune, or found a scorpion, he would tell us more. We were a large group of all different ages, trekking together. As I was one of the youngest and fittest, I spent a lot of time at the front of the group with Mohammed and another young man called Chris. We would run off from time to time, up and down the sand dunes. Mohammed would shout after us, telling us to preserve our energy and drink more water.

"Why are you always moving so fast? Slow down! Appreciate things," again, wise words.

Camels carried our backpacks, which contained clothes, sleeping bags and pillows. I carried a rucksack containing a first aid kit, spare socks, a camelback full of water and two extra water bottles, rehydration sachets, Kendall mint cake, snack bars, my camera, notebook, mobile phone, toilet roll and a plastic bag for putting used toilet roll into. Alongside Mohammed, Andy, an English ex-military guide, helped us along the trek. He took us through some stretches each morning and brought up the rear of the group. If we had any problems or concerns, we'd go to him for advice. A doctor called Jacqui completed the team of support staff in attendance.

On our first day in the desert, one lady had to drop out due to a sudden injury. By day three, a couple of trekkers were already suffering with the effects of heat exhaustion. I was determined to look after myself and not succumb, so I drank water all the time, being very careful to top up with rehydration sachets throughout the day. I felt fit and well, and I enjoyed everything the desert had to offer.

Surprisingly, you can get mobile phone signal in the desert, but only at certain points. Mum had been very concerned about me going away to complete the trek, and I'd left her in charge of Cilla, so I called her whenever I could for reassurance.

My favourite memory from the desert is the time we climbed Chegaga, the largest sand dune, then looked down the 100 metres over the sand from the top. I thought about Bobe, the reason I was doing this, and cried. A lady called Anne, who was in the early stages of Parkinson's Disease herself, was bravely trekking with us. We both proudly put on our charity T-shirts and had a photo taken together at the top of the dune. I hoped the money we had raised would help many others who were battling this horrible disease.

On our second-to-last day in the desert we were due to walk through the mirages and saltpans. I woke up that morning and stretched. My legs were a little heavy, which was no surprise considering how far I'd been walking in the heat. I unzipped my tent to go and find a cup of tea; always needed to start my day. It felt chilly, and I turned back to grab a jumper before joining the others at the breakfast station.

"Isn't it cold?" I said to Andy,

"No" he replied abruptly, giving me a strange look. "Go and grab some water." I took his advice, although I felt I wanted to warm up with numerous cups of tea instead. He kept his eye on me through our morning stretches and asked how I was feeling. I told him that my legs were a little sore, but it was nothing too bad.

"Keep drinking water and have an extra hydration sachet," he commanded. I obeyed.

We started walking and within about half an hour, I had fallen to the back of the group beside Andy.

"My legs really hurt," I told him.

He asked me to lie down and performed some deep stretches on them. They helped a little, but my legs were like jelly. We continued to walk slowly.

Out of nowhere, I had a strong urge to defecate. There are obviously no toilets in the desert, so our rules were that when we needed to go, we went off to the side of the group or hung behind a little and everyone just averted their eyes. I stayed back, then my stomach exploded. Julia, a fellow trekker, stayed behind with me and held my arm to keep me upright. I started crying, "I feel awful," I told her. "How can I continue?"

A few minutes later I was being violently sick. Andy made some phone calls.

"We'll just wait here," he told me, and a few minutes later a jeep pulled up. My heart sank. I had wanted to complete every mile of the trek, but the realisation dawned on me that I had heat exhaustion and could not walk any further. My legs just wouldn't hold me. I viewed the saltpans through the windows of the jeep with tears in my eyes.

I was taken to a large tent, where I lay down and fell asleep. Sometime later, I opened my eyes to find the rest of the group had emerged. I still didn't have the energy to lift my head, but a couple of them came over to speak to me and offered me water. They took it in turns to have camel rides at this stop point and I watched them from my horizontal position on the floor of the tent. I started to feel a little better, but Andy had made the decision that I would continue on in the jeep to night camp. I was able to chat to the driver more through this part of the drive, as well as take in the beautiful, shimmering mirages. I started to accept what had happened and told myself to be proud about getting as far as I did. When I arrived home and told people what had happened, none of them withheld their sponsorship and they agreed I'd done a great job.

The next day, we were taken by jeep to our hotel in Marrakesh. It was an extremely bumpy ride and no good for my still slightly-upset stomach. After freshening up, we went out to explore what the city had to offer. After eight days in the peaceful desert, I found it loud, busy and slightly scary. People approached us from all angles, trying to sell us their wares, encourage us into shops or put a chained monkey on our shoulder. We found a place to relax and eat, and, as I had started feeling better, I had a glass of wine. That evening, we continued drinking and smoking hookah pipes in the restaurant where we ate as a group one final time.

I left Morocco the next day, longing for more adventure, and started looking up other treks that I could complete with the same travel company as soon as I arrived home. I had always wanted to go on safari in Africa, so trekking through the Rift Valley with the Maasai in Tanzania, followed by four days of safari, sounded perfect. I just needed a means to fund it.

After mulling it over, I announced to my parents over dinner one evening, "I'm going to sell all my magic props and go on safari in Tanzania."

"What if you decide you want to go back into magic though? It's only been a year, and you might want to do pantomime again if you were offered it," Mum cautioned.

"No, I've thought it through. I don't want to go back to that. I can't see the good old days of variety in the theatres ever coming back. Plus, I can't swan off to pantomime for a month now that I have Cilla to consider and a job with a contract."

Mum made it clear that she thought it was a rash decision, but respected my choice. Dad, on the other hand, who was probably fed up of mending, painting and hauling props around, agreed with me that I should do what I wanted to do.

I advertised the props both individually and as a job lot on a magic website, and sure enough a man contacted me for more details. Eventually, he offered to collect the lot for a sum that would get me to Tanzania. Once I had the money, I wasted no time in booking and getting things ready for the trek in November 2012.

Tanzania felt really exciting. I'd lost the nerves that I had when I first flew to Africa with a group of strangers the year before. I also didn't have the added pressure of completing the trek for charity: this was just for me. I met with the group at the airport and we got on like a house on fire. Our first night was spent in a hotel, but the next morning we were taken up into the mountains in jeeps. We all had a few drinks and, truth be told, I didn't feel 100 percent fabulous the next day as we drove up into the Rift Valley mountains. However, I drank lots of water and enjoyed the sights through the windows: ladies carrying huge pots on their heads, children playing in the mud at the roadside, shacks selling fruit and vegetables, and even the occasional monkey. As we headed upwards and away from civilization, we saw herds of buffalo and impala. Tanzania was a whole new world, and it was love at first sight.

The jeeps dropped us off at our starting point and raced ahead with our belongings to set up for night camp. Our first day of trekking was short, about four hours, as we'd needed a fair bit of time to get up into the mountains. From the start the terrain was hilly, as you might expect. I had trained for this trek though and was happy to take on the challenges. I was slower than I'd been before, and I wondered if that was because there was so much more to take in than there had been in the desert. I stopped to take photos constantly, because it was so beautiful. I was soon at the back of the group, feeling short of breath, walking with one other lady and one of the Tanzanian guides. He offered to take my backpack for me.

"No!" I snapped at him uncharacteristically.

"He's trying to steal my bag," I whispered to the lady who was walking alongside me.

"No he's not, he's being helpful. You don't look all that well."

Once she'd pointed it out, I realised that yes, I felt weak. I started to drink more water. I couldn't have heat exhaustion already? Then I vomited.

Luckily we weren't far from camp. Ray, the guide, took my backpack and I walked with the expedition's doctor straight to my tent. I lay down, as I had a headache and wanted to go to sleep, but she warned me against this. She took my pulse rate and said it was high, before explaining that I had altitude sickness. We now had a big decision to make: I could either stay on the mountain and hope it wore off, or they could try to take me back down to the hotel. There were risks with taking me back; night was falling and it would be more difficult for the drivers to spot charging buffalo. I desperately wanted to complete the trek, so I told her I would stay put. She gave me some anti-sickness tablets and I spent the start of the evening being kept awake and throwing up intermittently while everyone else ate their dinner. I have never felt so poorly or been so scared. When the sickness had ceased, after a couple of hours, she let me drift off to sleep.

The next morning, I awoke feeling full of energy and excitement to start the day. I ate a massive breakfast and laughed and joked with the rest of the group. I did a nine-hour trek that day. The doctor was amazed, but said altitude sickness sometimes goes as quickly as it comes. I made sure to drink lots of water and consume hydration sachets to be on the safe side, but I was as fit as a fiddle once more. Ray, the guide, was never far from my side, asking how I was and checking that I didn't have the symptoms again. I apologised to him for my rudeness the day before. Confusion is another symptom of altitude sickness, and it certainly wasn't like me at all.

Our trek leader from the UK was a girl called Emma, who was full of fun. Stretches and warm ups in the morning became games and songs: we were even singing baby shark in the Rift Valley seven years before it became a hit in the UK! When she found out that I was a dance teacher, she tried to persuade me to lead some warm ups too, but I reminded her that this was my holiday and I was happy to join in with her and relax. In addition to Emma and the doctor, we had three guides from the tour company in Moshi (Ray and two others) plus about five Maasai guides who spoke no English, but sang, smiled and communicated with us in other ways. One of the guides carried a gun with him in case we got into trouble with prey animals, although the chances were apparently slim. Once again, toileting occurred at the back of the group, or off to the side, and we all averted our eyes. Dinners were vegetarian every night, much to my delight, as meat would have gone off in the heat. Each night seemed to be some variation on plantain stew. I'd never eaten plantain before, and I absolutely loved it: our stomachs suffered with the quantities that we were eating though! In the morning, we drank a chocolate malted drink called 'Milo' that I'd never heard of before, but was very popular in Tanzania: it took over from my tea obsession for the two weeks that I was there.

The Rift Valley takes your breath away. It's vast. There are different incredible views around every corner, and there are waterfalls and rivers you can swim in. It is a volcanic region, so we got covered in black ash throughout the trek. This, combined with the cream we applied because of the intense sun, caused us to end up extremely mucky each day. At camp each night, we'd be given a small bowl of water to try and wash as much off as we could. We visited a village in the middle of the region and were able to look around their mud hut homes for a small fee. I was amazed to see that inside there was room for a family and a goat. They had a fireplace to keep warm when temperatures dipped at night. The children were excited to see us, and we gave them gifts of stationery for school. We'd been told to give this instead of sweets, which would rot their teeth in a community where dental hygiene is not a priority.

We went to see one of their schools and were told by the guides that the children would walk for an hour or more in the mornings just to get there, as they are so spread out and there is no transport. It was a simple school, with a blackboard and children of different ages in the same class, but they were incredibly happy, sang to us and had their pictures taken. They were so beautiful and full of joy, despite having nothing at all. I thought of the children back in the UK, upset when they couldn't have the latest XBox game, and wondered where it all went wrong. There is so much to be happy about in life when we keep things simple.

We made campfires some evenings and toasted marshmallows. The Maasai guides treated us to a display of jumping, a traditional dance for them. They keep their arms by their sides and jump so high. It's really a sight to behold. They made jewellery out of beads and animal bones, which they sold to us at very low prices. My favourite souvenirs from my trek were the paintings that they made on sheets. I have one that depicts an elephant mother and baby, and another of the Maasai in their colourful dress holding their sticks.

When our trek was complete, we were taken into the city of Moshi so that we could see urban life and have a night out. Tanzanians know how to party! One of the guides collected us from our hotel in a pickup truck, and we all sat in the back with no seatbelts. We arrived at a bar, where everyone was drinking cocktails and dancing outside to African music. It was one of the best nights out I have ever had.

Our last four days in Tanzania were spent on safari, which was everything I had dreamed of. We completed one safari on foot, and saw buffalo, birds, and a huge lake of flamingo. The last three days were jeep safaris, during which time we ventured into the Ngorongoro crater. I'd waited all my life for this and finally, I was here. Tears sprung to my eyes as I saw the beauty all around me. I felt a sense of belonging and, despite being confined to a jeep, a deep sense of freedom. The jeep drove slowly and came to a halt every so often so we could take photos and watch the animals around us. Zebra crossing our path, followed by hundreds of gnu, who would parade in front of us, owning their land. Elephant families stayed close together and locked trunks occasionally. We saw eagles, ostrich, impala, giraffe, warthog and even some rhino from a distance. Then, there they were, sprawling lazily in the sun in the middle of the road. I watched and adored them: the lions of Tanzania. My heart beat to their tune and my soul soared with their roar. I posed for a photo, half out of the jeep's window, not feeling any fear at the sight of these magnificent creatures. We had come across a group of young males, who were resting in the sun, while looking to start their own pride. We saw several more lions during our days there, stalking buffalo and elephants, and even observed one chasing a zebra up a hill. Luckily for me, we did not see the gruesome end to that chase.

The other animals that fascinated me were the hippos. Hippos spend most of their day in the water to stay cool in the African sun, and because of their sensitive skin. We arrived at their pool to see just their eyes poking out from above the water. The guides told us not to get too close, because if they came after us they'd flatten us. Despite being vegetarian, hippos are one of the world's most dangerous animals, because they are territorial, strong and can tear up most animals with a single bite if they are provoked.

At the airport after two weeks in Tanzania, I cried my eyes out. I made a promise to this beautiful country that I would return. I couldn't even imagine going back to my ordinary life at home after this. I said a reluctant goodbye to Ray too, who had kept a close eye on me and ensured my safety after the altitude sickness on my first day. The magic of the Maasai and the spellbinding safari will stay in my heart forever. Until I can return...

Chapter 10 – Showgirls!

Towards the end of 2011, one of the teachers at Miss Marisa's needed some time off, so she asked if I could cover some extra classes in tap and street dance. I was really excited to do both, since they are my favourite styles of dance. We were working towards a show that would take place at the Princess Theatre in November 2012, which was a great experience for the children and good fun for the adult participants. In preparation, I put together some routines for my students that would work well on the stage.

One of my senior street dance students really stood out. She shone; not just with natural dance ability, but with a smile that would light up any stage. Becky reminded me a little bit of a young me, which made me want to inspire her and push her to get more out of dance. Whenever I demonstrated a move that made the others go, "I can't do that," Becky would give it a go. She had her own unique style, and she was a model student in every way.

The ballet students were performing a version of 'Peter Pan', and Marisa asked me if I would be their Captain Hook. I agreed and started rehearsals with the other principal cast members, one of whom was Lydia, a 15-year-old Australian girl who had dedicated herself to pointe and was playing the part of the crocodile. Another was Hayley, who was completing her teacher training at the time and would often shadow us in the studio. Hayley was a beautiful ballerina and made the perfect Tinkerbell. We had a lot of fun with our scenes.

As I got to know them, Becky, Hayley and Lydia asked if they could join my Just Jhoom! Bollywood classes. I had no objection, as they were all older students. I started wondering whether we could put a Bollywood routine into the November show, and Marisa loved the idea.

For Mum's birthday in February 2012, we took her to an Indian restaurant called Simla Spice. It was a big restaurant with a great atmosphere, and the waiters bantered with us all night and gave us free drinks. We all had fun and promised to come back soon.

"My daughter teaches Bollywood dance," Mum told the manager.

"No, you can't do that. How would you learn to dance like that?"

"I'll show you," I said. Mum, who had attended several classes and had decided to complete the Just Jhoom! training later that year, stood up with me and we performed some moves to the music that was playing in the restaurant. The manager looked on in shock.

"How about we put together a themed night for you, with dancers and an opportunity for your customers to learn some Bollywood?" Mum asked. He was excited and shared his phone number.

I talked to Hayley, Becky, Lydia and another dancer called Elysia about putting together some dances to perform at the restaurant. They all thought it was a fun opportunity, so we set a date with the manager of Simla Spice and a monthly 'Bollywood night' was born.

'Bollywood night' started with customers being taught the mudras (hand positions) used in traditional Indian dancing. Then they would learn an easy routine and follow along with a couple of others that we chose. After the class, they'd be encouraged to sit down and select their starter and main course options, and we would perform a few routines while they waited for their food to arrive. Between the starter and main course, we would again perform some lively routines in colourful costumes we had borrowed from Marisa. Then, between the main and dessert courses, we'd perform our final set.

The dressing room at the restaurant was one of the small female toilets, and the five of us would squash in and get ready together. We were paid £20 each and as much curry as we could eat. The audience was usually made up of a few tables of our family and friends who saw it as a monthly night out, as well as some Simla Spice regulars and holiday-makers. A journalist came to see what we were up to, and we got some great reviews in the local paper.

Next up was Marisa's show in November. Peter Pan the ballet went really well, and I loved getting into character as Captain Hook. My street dance students, adult tap class and musical theatre performers also did really well and got great applause from their family and friends. The Princess Theatre has a huge stage, but everyone was really excited, which distracted them from any nerves they may have had.

Our next performance, at the end of November, was slightly more nerve-wracking for me. Mum asked if the five of us who had performed at Bollywood night would be able to put together a couple of routines for her major showcase event. She said she may be able to get us some more work from it, if that's what we wanted to do. I was amazed she had even considered this, with our little troupe from the dance school, and when I spoke to the other girls, they were excited. Unfortunately, Elysia was away at this time, but Hayley, Becky, Lydia and I were available to perform. My friend Zoe also stepped in to cover as a fifth person for the Bollywood routines. We opened the show with a funky street routine, which Hayley started en pointe, then opened the second half with a Bollywood medley. It went really well, and lots of Mum's clients, who I'd got to know over the years working in the agency and performing as a cabaret, came up to congratulate me on my new venture.

Work started coming in for the next summer season – some corporate, Indian-themed events and some holiday centre shows. For these, we had decided we could perform a mixture of styles, including Bollywood, street, cheer, ballet and tap. We were able to incorporate some audience participation and fun too, as I was no stranger to chatting on a microphone. At holiday centres, we were generally booked to run a short street dance workshop at the beginning of the evening for the children, and they became part of the show with us, performing the track they had learnt.

We rehearsed once or twice a week after classes, at Marisa's studio or in my living room, and all of us gave some creative input for the main show.

We were asked for publicity photos, which would help the venues where we were performing to advertise us. My friend Rebecca is a talented, creative photographer, and she was able to capture us wearing our various costumes in different locations and poses. She wanted to photograph us in the middle of a road, so I vividly remember running into the highway, posing or jumping for an action shot, then running out of the way again as we heard a car approaching. We got some great shots and chose one with each of us wearing a different outfit, representing the dance styles we performed, to use as our main picture. Rebecca added our logo to this, which enhanced our professional look.

For the holiday centres, our show would start with 'Don't Stop the Party' or 'Party Rock Anthem', and we'd burst onto the stage in a blaze of bright-orange tracksuit bottoms and 'So Street' logo tops, jumping around and break dancing. We always finished the show with our ballet/street mash up in sparkly hoodies, as well as these trademark orange tracksuit bottoms. In between, we'd wear tailcoats for tap and skirts and vest tops with logos on for cheer. Lydia and Hayley had black and white tutus for ballet, and we all had multi coloured, jewelled outfits for Bollywood. Audiences loved it, as it was something really different.

Behind the scenes, we were always full of fun and banter. We became close friends who could pick each other up after a bad day, and had several in-jokes and sayings. Becky was still only 15-years-old and by far the smallest, so we nicknamed her 'Baby Jhoom!' We even managed to fit her into a tumble dryer while waiting for the show to start at a holiday park on one occasion. Hayley and I once replaced the Dandiya Garba sticks, which we used to dance with at our 'Bollywood nights', with sticks of rhubarb. No one noticed this, but we were all greatly entertained. We even had a bear mascot called Rhubarb, named after this instance, who we took to shows with us. We'd got him from 'Build a Bear', and when you squeezed his tummy you'd hear us singing, 'A Hustler's Work is Never Through' which was part of the David Guetta song 'Play Hard', that we sometimes used in the show.

One of our favourite shows was at a Bollywood-themed wedding, where everyone was dressed up in full regalia. We taught them a routine, then performed some of our favourite dances.

Another memorable performance was at a holiday centre in Looe, which we visited regularly in the summer holidays. I knew the entertainments manager well, a man named Captain Crumble, from when I'd performed my magic shows at different parks that he'd worked on. We always had a good laugh with him, and we even started incorporating the song 'Copacabana' into the show to satisfy his love for Barry Manilow. (Years later, I joined him at a Manilow concert – it was fabulous!) On this occasion, we arrived in Looe in good time – I always made sure we were early when it came to shows – and started getting ready. I unpacked my bag, only to realise that I'd left behind the tablet with all our music on it. We'd travelled in Hayley's car, so she went out to check if she had a CD copy of the show in her car, as often we listened to it and rehearsed in our heads on our way. Of course, today she did not.

"Ami, take a look through my CDs, surely you can throw something together," said Crumble in his cheerful cockney accent, thinking optimistically about the situation. The problem as I saw it was that we'd cut and mixed a lot of tracks especially for the show, and the routines were set to these.

We had an hour to get something together, so the girls searched through Crumble's CDs. Hayley instantly found 'Party Rock Anthem' and Lydia located 'Dance With Me Tonight', a number they performed their ballet routine to. I was worried about finding Bollywood music, but stumbled across the Pussycat Dolls version of 'Jai Ho!' on a CD. We couldn't find 'Shake it Off', our cheer track, but found 'Hot and Cold', which we'd used before for an event, so we were able to go through that. We also found a track for the end routine with the same beat as the track we were using, so we simply improvised, applying our dances to new music. Within an hour, with a random CD collection, we'd managed to save the show. We performed that night and it was one of the best shows we ever had, with massive applause and children asking for our autographs at the end.

Occasionally, we'd have two shows in the same area and would stay overnight at the holiday centres to avoid travelling the next day. This meant we could have some drinks with the team, or sometimes take part in karaoke. One week, we were performing in Padstow one night and Looe the next, so we asked if we could stay in Padstow and were told that everything would be fine.

"Do we need to bring anything?" I asked.

"No, we have everything in our cabaret van," came the reply.

We had taken Cilla with us on this occasion, as both parks were dog friendly and it meant we could get her out for walks on the gorgeous Cornish beaches in the day. We travelled down to Padstow and checked out the van, so we could put on our makeup and chill out in there before the show. As the senior members of the crew, Hayley and I ran to bag the double room. It was made up with a single duvet, but we assumed there must be more bedding in the other rooms. There was not. We had a single duvet between the four of us, and although it was summer, it was not warm enough to sleep without bedding. I went to reception and asked if they had any more, but no luck.

I phoned Mum, who is always resourceful, and told her our predicament.

"There's a Shearings hotel in Newquay, perhaps they can put you up for the night," she said. We were in luck, they would give us two rooms at staff rates; but they had a 'no dogs' policy. Cilla was generally pretty quiet, so we decided this wasn't a problem. When we arrived there just before midnight, Lydia smuggled her in under her oversized hoodie, after which we just had to hope she didn't bark when we went down for our breakfast! Luckily, we got away with it and enjoyed a relaxed, sunny day on the beach before our show that evening.

We worked together performing this show and many others, for four years. Another three dancers were introduced to the So Street crew during this time, in case any one of us was away or unable to perform, or if we needed an extra member for a big event. Lauren and Megan were recommended via a fellow dance teacher, and I got a message online from another Amy (Amy II, as we called her) asking if she could join the troupe. I scheduled a meeting with her, checked out some videos of previous performances, and was excited for her to join us. They all became great assets and friends, bringing their own style to the shows. I always chose dancers to join us based on the following: great dance ability, willingness to get involved in whatever crazy shows we were creating, and a fun personality on stage. They didn't have to be the thinnest or tallest. I had decided to always promote body positivity and run the crew for fun predominantly, rather than basing everything on profit.

This ethos meant we were happy to get involved in local charity events and carnivals, which helped us to promote ourselves while supporting a good cause, but mainly because we loved dancing at any opportunity we were given. We would warm-up the walkers at an annual charity night walk event for a local hospice. Even during the Covid-19 lockdown, I recorded a video warm up for them. The event is usually themed, so we embraced the opportunity to dress up as cowgirls, showgirls, pirates or in 80s or 90s themed outfits. One year, we completed the walk with the participants after delivering five warm-up sessions! We were really tired after that.

There was never any competition between us. We were all unique in style and became each other's cheerleaders; we never fell out. As for little Becky, I wanted her first professional performances and experiences of dancing work to be good ones that inspired her to do bigger things.

As I noted at the start of this book, nothing makes me feel better than dancing on stage. The summer of 2013 was so much fun, and we performed shows most weeks. Those lovely girls contributed in their own ways to helping me through what ended up being a really hard year.

Chapter 11 – Systems Down

In March 2013, tragedy struck our family again. My paternal Grandad suffered a stroke and was rushed into hospital. We were told that he'd lost part of his brain function, was unlikely to ever recover completely, and was also at risk of having a second stroke. I travelled with my parents to Sheffield to see him in the hospital. Grandad had always been lively, energetic and fun. He walked all of the neighbourhood dogs and rode a motorbike well into his 80s, so it was strange to see him in a hospital bed, unable to speak properly. He knew we were there though, and he held a conversation with us through hand signals. We came back to Torquay that evening, but got the news a couple of days later that Grandad had suffered a second stroke and wasn't doing well. Dad drove back up to be with him and Grandma. A couple of days later we got the news that he had passed away. It all happened so quickly. There was no time to prepare ourselves as we had, in a way, with Bobe. I was glad he hadn't gone through the prolonged suffering she had, but it was a shock that he had just gone so quickly.

We had booked a family holiday to Mallorca in April, which both Grandad and Grandma, alongside Mum, Dad, my Aunty Pamela, my maternal Grandad and I were all supposed to be going on. We were worried about the effect this would have on my Grandma, so shortly after Grandad's passing, but we also felt it would be nice for her to be with the family and have some time away from home. She enjoyed parts of it, but it was a difficult holiday for her.

It was also a difficult holiday for me, as I was coming to terms with some home truths. I stood in front of the mirror in my parent's hotel room one evening before dinner, staring at my reflection. I was adjusting my hair and mascara, breathing in and out,

"Do I look fat in this Mum?"

"No Ami, because you are not fat," she said, exasperated. "You're becoming a bit obsessed asking me these questions all the time."

It was true. I was constantly looking in the mirror trying to find fault with myself. I did several dance classes a week, saw a personal trainer and ate quite healthily, but still felt that I was fat and ugly to look at. I was weighing myself several times a day, and if I put on a pound I would cry and beat myself up, telling myself over and over again that I was disgusting. I'd slap myself and tell myself I wasn't worthy of love and would never find a boyfriend. There were times at home when I was meant to be going for a night out with friends and had to cancel, because I couldn't get my hair quite right. I distinctly remember one evening, after I'd done my hair and makeup, that I smudged my eyeliner slightly and broke down crying about it. I got in the shower to wash it all off and re-do my hair, then re-did everything and still couldn't go out. I looked at myself in the full length mirror in my bedroom and saw an overweight person looking back at me.

"If you go out wearing that dress everyone will laugh at you," my inner voice told me. "It's too clingy, you look ridiculous." I couldn't bear to be seen in public unless I wore baggy clothes. This wasn't new; it had been getting worse and worse over the months, but Mallorca and my Mum speaking out to me proved to be the tipping point. Sure, my friends had been concerned before, when I'd not been able to go out with them or they'd turned up at my house to find me drunk and in tears, but when Mum said it, it finally it hit home.

We got back to England and I told Mum I would make an appointment to see my GP. Work was so busy though; I used that to try and take my mind off things and put off seeing him. I was learning quickly in my new HR role and still teaching around ten classes per week. That's when I started having thoughts about how life was so unpredictable and wondered why I was here at all. I was driving home one evening and suddenly had a really strong desire to drive my car into the wall ahead of me. I fantasised about people finding the wreck with me in it. Then, I looked at Cilla on the passenger seat, and I knew I couldn't do that to her.

I lay in bed one night, counting in my head the number of tablets I had in the house – some were quite strong, prescribed to me for back pain. I thought about taking them and just drifting away. Again, my thoughts turned to Cilla and her epilepsy - who would look after her if I was gone?

I scared myself with these thoughts, so I finally made an appointment to see my GP. I poured everything out to him: all the self-loathing, my low self-esteem, the suicidal ideation. I had also been picking the skin on my scalp whenever I felt low and had made it bleed a couple of times. My GP listened and made lots of notes. He then told me he thought I may have depression and body dysmorphia, but would like to refer me to a psychiatrist for a proper diagnosis. He questioned whether I was bulimic, with all the exercise I did too, but I assured him that most of that was essential for my job. He asked if I would like to start on some anti-depressants in the meantime, but I refused as I wanted to do some research first – the thought of taking tablets for my mood scared me.

My referral letter came through really quickly: the appointment with the psychiatrist was only a couple of weeks after seeing my GP. While I waited, I read up on the internet as much as I could about body dysmorphic disorder. The symptoms described were pretty similar to mine: obsessing constantly about a certain body part or parts, trying to hide or 'fix' these parts and being unable to do some day-to-day activities due to obsession. I was certainly obsessed with my weight and how my stomach and hair looked, and I was sometimes late to work due to a preoccupation with my appearance. I had stopped being as social, because it meant I could hide out at home. Skin picking was also a major symptom for many people. I thought it was a start to at least identify the problem: now I knew I could be helped, I just had to work on myself. I looked forward to my psychiatrist appointment.

However, when I arrived for my appointment the psychiatrist was looking down, tapping on her keyboard, and didn't make any effort to make me feel comfortable. She had black curly hair and glasses, and I felt like an inconvenience to her.

"So, what's the problem?" she asked in a thick foreign accent.

I begrudgingly went through my symptoms and she told me that it sounded like the GP had it right – depression and body dysmorphic disorder. She said I would need to start a course of Fluoxetine and see her weekly for therapy sessions.

"Fluoxetine is Prozac - I don't want to take that," I told her. I'd done my research on different psychotherapeutic drugs since speaking to my GP, and clips from the film 'Prozac Nation' filled my head.

"You have to take something for me to treat you, or I cannot have you as a patient," she told me. I knew I'd been lucky to get this appointment, and I wanted to get better, but at the time I was strong in my opinion that I did not want to take the drugs. I left feeling deflated, having been told I could not be helped.

My friend Zoe, who worked as a Mental Health Social Worker, came over that night and I told her what had happened with the psychiatrist.

"Ami, you need to take those tablets. Let me explain it to you. When someone's brain is wired wrongly, it needs rest and intervention so it can be rewired. It's all very good having conversational therapy, but without the drugs to switch off the parts of your brain that are firing wrongly, you won't take on the advice to help make it right." I listened with interest. It suddenly made perfect sense. Why hadn't the psychiatrist explained it in this way?

I called the GP the next day and explained everything to him. I asked if I could be re-referred, but he said no, as it was a busy waiting list and he'd had to pull strings to get me on in the first place. However, he could provide the Fluoxetine if I'd like to start on it. I agreed.

I hadn't been keen on the unfriendly psychiatrist anyway, and Mum had told me if we could find someone privately then she would help with the cost of my sessions.

When Bobe died, I went through a few sessions of counselling with a lady a friend had suggested to me, as she'd helped her when someone close had passed away. I got on well with the counsellor and found the sessions useful, so I looked her up again and explained my situation. She told me she'd be able to work with me using EMDR (eye movement desensitisation and reprocessing), EFT (emotional freedom technique) and hypnotherapy practices. I had nothing to lose, so I booked in to see her the following week.

Starting Fluoxetine was frightening for me. I'd read up on all the possible side effects and wondered how I would feel. At first, I didn't notice much of a difference, but as time went on I just felt dreadfully tired all the time. I fell asleep in meetings at work and couldn't stay awake past 9p.m. most nights. Luckily, my employers were very understanding of my situation. If I needed time off they granted it, and Syra suggested that one of my four days a week be worked on the yard for the time being, so I could get some fresh air and movement. I was so grateful to them. Jerry had also decided to invest in some training for me, so I started my CIPD Level 3 HR course at the local college, one day a week from September 2013. I loved my training, but again, I was falling asleep in classes. My tutor and peer group understood, and I'd try doing star jumps if I was tired in class to perk me up. I had one friend on the course who even went so far as to call me on college mornings to make sure I was awake and got there on time! I also ate piles of biscuits to try and keep me on a sugar high.

I went on holiday to Gambia with my friend Nikki in January 2014, which was really good for me. On the trip we went on a gentle morning canoe ride in a beautiful location where the birds were singing. However, Nikki had to keep waking me up, shaking me and saying I needed to stay awake so that I didn't capsize the canoe. I could literally sleep anywhere.

Therapy went well. I was able to talk through where my self-loathing had started. Growing up in a show business family, there had always been an expectation I put on myself to look a certain way. My role models – Mum, her assistants and even Bobe always wore a lot of makeup and looked glamorous 24/7. Then, I'd been bullied through school and in my first Q'dos tour. I was used to being backstage with people who were tiny, complaining that they were fat. My whole idea of a healthy weight was completely warped. I was striving to look perfect, when actually there was no such thing as perfection. I also had deep personal difficulties in thinking back to my childhood and my biological father. I still could not understand why he had no interest in me, and I often wondered what I had done wrong. Mum worked long hours when I was little, to make ends meet and ensure we always had a roof over our heads, so I'd been left with different nannies who cared for me. My therapist thought I had attachment issues, which explained why losing grandparents who I was so close to was the trigger that caused my mental health challenges to explode. She recorded tapes for me to listen to in the evenings. I'd lie with my eyes closed and listen to her soothing voice telling me I was worthy of love, that I was enough just as I am. My brain started to take on these messages, little by little.

I decided to get rid of my bathroom scales, which I'd developed such an intense love-hate relationship with. I also got rid of the mirror in my bedroom, so I just had a small one in the bathroom for doing my makeup in and a full-length one by the front door. This stopped me from looking at myself so often. I'd get up, pull on some clothes, do my makeup and get out. I put time limits on it – ten minutes in front of the bathroom mirror, get the job done, no obsessing.

I completed my therapy and started reducing my tablets slowly, under the GP's advice, until finally I was off them in just under a year. This may seem quick to anyone who has used antidepressant medication, but I was so determined to get better and had set a goal in my head to not be on them for longer than a year. While mental illness is a process to get through, just like any illness, I feel that both can be conquered with crazy determination alongside the right treatment and support. I hated the Fluoxetine, but after that year I was convinced that the tablets had, together with the therapy, saved my life.

As I came off my tablets, Cilla ended up on her own course of medication, designed to help control her epilepsy. She had been having seizures more frequently, and the vet advised that the time had come. I'd been reluctant at first, as any medications could give her unwanted side effects, and she was still so young. I also knew that the more seizures she had, the more prone she would be to brain damage, so I eventually agreed. She started off well on them and the frequency of the seizures reduced.

In the midst of that crazy year, I'd been contacted by a man I had worked with at the Torbay Hotel. He wanted to take me out on a date. I wasn't sure at first, considering what I was going through, but eventually decided that it couldn't do me any harm. In fact, he was very complimentary about me and I thought dating could be fun, so I agreed to meet him for a meal in December 2013. We got on well and had several subsequent dates. I was always upfront with people about my mental health, and he was very supportive of that. We continued to date until March 2014, when he was offered a promotion with his job that entailed moving to another part of the country. Suddenly I had a big decision to make.

Chapter 12 – Moving On Up

We entered the hotel lobby and were greeted by a smiling man with glasses who, despite us having never met him, seemed to know who we were. He checked us in and showed us to our suite. It was beautiful – a huge, four-poster bed sat in the centre of the room, while there was also an en suite bathroom and a lounge area off to the left with a window that looked out over the grounds. The minute the man left the room I threw myself on to the bed and declared, "I'm home!"

"We won't be living in this room, Ami."

"I know, but I love the place, and the feel of it all."

We'd arrived at the hotel where my partner had been offered the assistant manager's role, for us to check it out and for him to consider if he'd like to take the job. I was undecided about moving. After all, I was settled at the Mare and Foal Sanctuary, had my lovely little house, and my family and friends were all in the Torbay area. However, now we'd arrived, I was warming to the idea of a new start. I could look into teaching some dance classes here and find some other part-time work, possibly even within the hotel. I would easily be able to rent out my house, and the position came with a flat anyway, so we could live in the hotel grounds. I would be able to devote more time to my studying without the extra pressure of paying my mortgage each month.

We freshened up from the drive and took Cilla for a walk in the National Trust grounds, just across the road from the hotel. The area seemed perfect for her –

lots to see and sniff. She wagged her tail and enjoyed her expedition. That afternoon, my partner had a meeting with the hotel manager to talk through how the hotel ran and what the position would entail, so Cilla and I took a longer walk around the village, which was located just outside of Stratford-upon-Avon. As we would be staying overnight, we planned to visit Stratford itself the next day. Dinner in the hotel was impressive – this was not your average Shearings accommodation. The premises had been bought as a more upmarket addition to the chain, and it delivered. They even allowed Cilla to sit in with us at dinner time, as we explained about her epilepsy. Nothing was too much trouble for anyone.

The next morning we enjoyed our breakfast, which was followed by a riverside walk and some sightseeing in the town. I loved the quirky buildings and the fact that we would be so near to The Globe Theatre. With this visit, I think my mind was made up.

We arrived home, and my partner accepted the job. He would be moving within a month, so I started looking for animal welfare jobs within the area. I didn't want to move or give notice until I'd found the right thing, but eventually a part-time job came up at the visitor centre of another equine welfare centre. I interviewed and was successful. I rented out my house to Hayley from 'So Street' and her partner, then moved myself and Cilla up to Stratford-upon-Avon. Our flat was lovely, nestled at the top of one of the buildings surrounding the hotel. This was an old farm, which consisted of a main farmhouse and several outhouses. We had a large bedroom, kitchen, lounge and bathroom. It was bigger than my house! Cilla settled in straight away. She enjoyed all the hotel employees fussing over her, as well as her huge new garden.

I started work at the equine sanctuary, a couple of days a week in May 2014. It wasn't all it was cracked up to be though. For a start, the manager of the sanctuary (with whom I'd had a great rapport during the interview) was leaving, and I didn't get on as well with her deputy. It was very different to the family-run Mare and Foal Sanctuary – this was more business-like, and visitor centre employees were not permitted to groom or attend to the ponies in their spare time. We didn't give tours around the site; customers were left to find their own way and big colourful signs gave them the information they needed, so we mainly just served food in the cafe and sold items in the gift shop. I got bored quickly and craved my Mare and Foal family. I spoke to Jerry on the phone at the end of June. He'd been unable to fill my position and said he would love to have me back, so I chatted with my partner and we agreed that I'd spend three days a week back in Torbay working at the sanctuary, then come to Stratford for the rest of the week to study and spend time with him. While in Torbay, I could stay in Grandad's spare room, so we were able to spend some extra time together. This also meant that I didn't have to pay out the money to rent somewhere, or go back to my house and pay the mortgage on top of travel. It was a three-hour drive, but I was used to long trips from my days travelling to gigs, so was happy to listen to music and enjoy the journey.

Everything worked well for some time, and my partner was very settled at the hotel, but I wondered how long I could sustain it for. I was looking for jobs, driving back and forth from Stratford to Torquay, for a total of four months. Then, a seasonal position drew my attention. I decided that although it was temporary, I owed it to myself to make the leap to see if we could make things work. Besides, I would be better placed looking for work in the area if I was actually there full time.

In October, I interviewed for the role of an elf in 'The Magical Journey', the brainchild of Laurence Llewelyn-Bowen. Then, in November, I found out I'd been successful. I had training and costume fitting later that month, before the attraction opened to the public. The concept was, in fact, magical. Visitors would arrive at a sparkling, 'snow-covered' dome where they were met by their elf guide and taken in groups of up to twenty people through the journey. Guests would meet 'Simon Cowelf' and 'Mummy Claus' in two separate rooms. These characters explained the plight of Santa, who had lost Rudy the Baby Reindeer, and needed their help in finding him in time for Christmas present deliveries. The families would then be escorted on to a train, which took them into the magical forest. Here, they'd gather in an igloo and be treated to hot chocolate while Jack Frost performed magic or juggled, or was joined by performers on stilts. One of the characters would also read the visitors a story. After this, the tour party was led through the forest to look for reindeer hoof prints, guided and encouraged by the different elves, until they reached a clearing where the reindeer stood. Rudy was there too, having found his way back on his own after all. The last part of the journey saw guests ushered to their own huts (one per family) to meet Santa, have their photograph taken and receive a gift. Finally, they'd return to the dome to collect their photo and have some hot snacks.

I've always been a fan of Christmas, I'm a big kid at heart, so I loved being a part of the excitement. I was able to really get into the elf character too. I normally escorted guests through the start of the journey, until they got onto the train, so I had developed my own routine and self-made script for that purpose. I loved seeing the children's eyes light up in wonder, and encouraged them to shout at Simon Cowelf when he suggested that toilet roll was a suitable Christmas gift.

Unfortunately, the general public did not feel the same way as me. They felt that the attraction was overpriced and not quite magical enough. An unflattering newspaper review prompted Laurence to close the journey down, so we got to work making the place even more Christmassy – more glitter, more fake snow, more performers and a second train. He really pulled out all the stops. Laurence was on site directing a lot of this, so I got to meet him too. When we reopened, visitors seemed a lot happier, which made me happy too, picking up extra shifts as I revelled in the excitement of it all.

During my first week at the Magical Journey, I managed to interview for a couple of positions with animal sanctuaries. I didn't get the position at Dog's Trust, but I was over the moon to get a receptionist position at RSPCA Coventry and Nuneaton. It was a 40-minute drive for me, but I didn't care as I'd be working with animals again, plus I really loved Sue and Glenn who interviewed me. When I walked into my interview a greyhound was standing on the table, so I knew it was going to be a good one! I started pretty quickly, again part-time, working two days a week. This was practical, because I could work it around my Magical Journey shifts. Sue showed me the ropes and soon enough I was taking calls, booking people in to see animals, filling in the paperwork if they took them home, booking in the rescued animals that came in to us, and selling the pet products in the shop. I was able to take Cilla to work with me occasionally, which was a massive bonus, and there were often other dogs or cats who hung out in reception with us, and even a hamster who I became quite attached to.

All the centre staff were lovely, enthusiastic and passionate about the animals. They were happy to answer my questions and to let me walk the dogs with them when it was quiet. We also had some fabulous volunteers, who would run home checks for the animals, then report back to us. There were two ladies who sold raffle tickets or ran other promotions in reception with us, and they made amazing cakes for us all.

I was able to really appreciate the work that the RSPCA does. The Coventry and Nuneaton branch is very small and independently-run, so although it has the RSPCA name, they do all their own fundraising and promotion. Therefore, staff were constantly coming up with ideas for community events and fundraisers, and it felt like a real team effort. We would still take in some animals from RSPCA inspectors though, who were often overworked and running around from place to place, getting to the animals who were most in need. At the centre, our waiting list would generally be 50-long for dogs and over 100-long for cats. It really highlighted to me how many people buy or take on animals that they can't look after. Often, they come to see them as a chore or don't put the time in to train them. Sometimes, people would get desperate, leaving boxes containing animals outside the shelter, and we'd find them in the morning. Once, a lady came in expecting to leave a cat that she couldn't take care of anymore. I explained that I would have to put the animal on the waiting list and went to take her details, but she simply threw the cat at me and ran. It was such a gorgeous, friendly cat too. I know that sometimes circumstances can be difficult, but I've always seen animals as family members, so I couldn't understand why people wouldn't move heaven and earth to keep them safe at home. Luckily, after being treated for fleas and worms, that cat was rehomed pretty quickly. It's not always the story for some, who wait a long time for adoption. The experience of working in animal welfare made me feel bad for buying Cilla from a breeder. I hadn't been educated at the time though, nor had I heard much about rescuing animals before. I made up my mind that my next dog would be a rescue.

I settled into a great routine with The Magical Journey and RSPCA. Sometimes I could go from one job to the other quite easily. My partner was able to take Cilla to work, so she was well cared for, and we were never short of hotel staff wanting to dog-sit for her if that didn't work out. I had made some good friends in both jobs, so my social life was great too.

Everything was going well until suddenly, in December, I started having second thoughts about my relationship. I decided that I'd see how things went over

Christmas and New Year. After all, I'd finally made my move up to Stratford and didn't want to be hasty.

The Magical Journey closed for a second and final time, just before Christmas. It was such a shame, because I thought it was a lovely attraction. We were all told one evening that it wouldn't be opening the next day, which was a massive blow for a lot of employees, who thought they'd have jobs into the new year. I was lucky enough to be able to pick up a few extra shifts at the RSPCA, while I'd also been contracted as the Entertainments Host at the hotel where we lived for the Christmas and New Year breaks. At this point, I hadn't done any hosting or singing for about three years, but it was like riding a bicycle. I got straight back into chatting with guests and doing everything I could to make their festive breaks special. We had some great cabaret acts too, which made things easier. When I did find the courage to sing at the end of the breaks, I discovered that my voice was certainly not as strong as it had once been, but I could still hold a tune. The audience, who had got to know me by this time, appreciated it. My parents and Grandad came up to stay for the New Year's break and enjoyed themselves too; we took them out to explore all our local haunts and walks. Mum asked me how things were going in my relationship though, as she could sense that things weren't right.

I confronted my partner about it at the end of January, when there was still no real improvement. In fact, I felt we'd drifted apart even more. I told him I felt we were more like friends sharing a flat than boyfriend and girlfriend. He was shocked at first, but after thinking it through, he seemed to agree. We decided that I'd stay for another month so I could give notice on my job. We were still getting on as friends after all.

I got a call from my friend Ollie, who was an illusionist from Milton Keynes. He told me he'd been asked to do a few gigs for Pontins in February and needed an assistant. As I would be unemployed by then, I told him I'd love to do it, so he came over to Stratford to rehearse with me in one of the hotel's big function rooms. It felt fun to be doing magic again, and I felt confident working with a friend and being the assistant, which eased some pressure. I also finally got a chance to perform the cardboard box illusion, which doesn't sound very impressive, but was something I'd always wanted to do. The magician picks up a flat-packed cardboard box and shows it to the audience, opening it out to show it is just a regular container. The assistant gets in, the box is closed and numerous wooden poles are shoved randomly through the cardboard box. It's such an effective illusion, because it really is just a cardboard box!

Ollie and I spent the February half-term break travelling around Pontins sites. It felt good to get away from the hotel with a friend and have some fun. I knew then that I'd made the right decision.

I now had several challenges in front of me, which fuelled my anxiety. I would need to go back to Torquay to tell everyone my relationship had broken up, which was tough after they had given us such a lovely going away party as a send off. I needed another job too, as Jerry had found a new assistant at the Mare and Foal Sanctuary. I also needed to give Hayley notice on my house, which I felt bad about since they'd been there for less than a year.

I felt like a bit of a failure.

Chapter 13 – Back in the Spotlight

"Hi Jerry."

"Oh Ames, how lovely to hear from you!" my cheery former boss chirped. "How are things with the boyfriend in Stratford?"

I tried to explain the situation as best I could, then got to the purpose of the call.

"I don't suppose there are any jobs going at the moment? On the yard or in one of the charity shops?"

"Funny you should ask about jobs. The girl we took on as your replacement walked out last week. Now, I'd need to check with Syra, as you've messed us around a bit going away, coming back, going away... but I'd be pleased to have you back if she will."

"Wow that would be amazing!" I exclaimed.

"OK darling, I'll speak to her and call you back."

I spent the next few hours holding my breath, wondering if everything could really work out so perfectly again. Jerry called back as he said he would,

"Syra says I can re-employ you. This is the last time though. No more running away with boyfriends."

I laughed and promised not to repeat the excursion. I was delighted and eager to see my human and equine friends again, especially Sumo. I settled back into Sanctuary life like I'd never been away.

About a month after we returned to Torquay, Cilla was attacked by another dog. We were out walking one morning while my car was in the garage, just passing our local newspaper shop. There, a dog sat quietly outside, obviously waiting for his owner to come out. I smiled at him, as I tend to do with dogs, and walked on by.

Before I knew what was happening, the dog ran up behind us, grabbed Cilla by the neck and started shaking her violently. I panicked, forgetting everything I'd ever been told about dog fights. I got down on the floor and tried to open his jaw with my hand, but he had locked it: instead of releasing Cilla, my hand was now stuck in his mouth too. I screamed for help and, after what felt like hours, a car pulled up and out jumped two ladies who tried to help us. One ran into the shop to find the owner, who came out, grabbed the dogs' legs, and managed to pull him away. The ladies ushered Cilla and I into their car, and I directed them to the vets. Meanwhile, the shop assistant took down the man's details. I was in severe pain myself, but called the vet through my tears and asked them to expect us imminently. I held Cilla on my lap and prayed that she'd be OK.

The vets instantly rushed Cilla into the examination room. I asked to go with her, but they told me they needed to look at her as soon as possible because of the injuries and blood loss. I sat in the waiting room and called Mum, who was there within minutes.

"Ami, we need to get you to the hospital. Your wounds are deep and you're losing a lot of blood."

"I'm not leaving Cilla," I told her stubbornly.

Eventually, the vet came out and invited us to go through to the consulting room. She explained to us that Cilla was extremely poorly, but assured us she was doing everything she could. Cilla was being treated for shock, on a drip with fluids and antibiotics, so she wasn't able to move much. The vet told me that I should go to the hospital to get myself some treatment, then come back later when she'd had a chance to review Cilla's progress.

"I'll go after I've seen Cilla."

"I don't recommend it, it may be upsetting."

I reminded the vet that I'd worked in animal welfare for years. I understood that Cilla was very unwell, but I needed to see her just in case it was our final goodbye. She gave in, so Mum and I walked into the back room to see our little dog lying motionless, hooked up to her drip. When she realised it was us, she gave a weak wag of her tail. Mum placed her hands lightly over her to give her some healing, and I held back my tears, wanting to give her hope rather than show her I was upset. When we left the room again, Mum squeezed my shoulder, "It will be okay," she whispered.

I hoped she was right. On the way to the hospital, I thought to myself that if Cilla didn't make it, neither would I. She had got me through my depression and thus saved my life several times. She was my best friend. We'd fought so hard through her epilepsy, and I couldn't lose her to this.

In the A&E department, adrenaline faded, pain finally kicked in, and I started screaming. They loaded me up on morphine, gave me a tetanus shot and bandaged my hand, but they couldn't put stitches in: if there was any infection, they'd be sealing it in. The medical staff told me that the dog may have bitten through some tendons, which would lead to permanent damage. To assess the injury and decide on potential physiotherapy treatment, I'd need to see my doctor in a couple of weeks.

As we left the hospital, I called the vet, who told me it wasn't good news. Cilla wasn't responding to treatment and they would be unable to stay with her overnight. The only option would be to take her to Cave, a veterinary specialist hospital in Wellington. Of course, we agreed, we would do anything for our family. We picked Cilla up, drip still attached, and Mum drove us for over an hour to the hospital. On the journey, I held the drip in the back with my good hand and comforted Cilla. We dropped her off, came home, and hardly slept all night.

The next morning the vet called to say we could go to see Cilla: she'd made it through the night. She was stable and eating, but she hadn't moved at all and it was possible that she had been paralysed. He told me the next 24 hours were critical, but to come and see her. We arrived at Cave and were escorted to a consultation room. The vet went to get Cilla, then returned and placed her on the floor. To my amazement, she promptly walked towards me. I giggled through my tears.

"She's not paralysed, just stubborn!"

She had responded to our love and prayers and fought through it for us.

Cilla underwent six weeks of cage rest and physio, towards the end of which she got very impatient and howled for walks. She made a full recovery, as did I, bar some scarring across my hand. We were both extremely lucky.

As it was coming towards the start of the summer season, Mum was able to find the 'So Street' troupe some work. We had put together a more suitable, classy act for the hotels, where we worked under the name 'Dynamique'. To start with, she booked us for a run every Wednesday night at The Esplanade Hotel in Paignton. The stage was small and it was a low-budget affair, so only three of us performed – usually Becky, Hayley and me. The show went down really well with the older age group.

We still picked up some occasional work on the holiday parks, at corporate events and outdoor festivals too. Mum asked us to choreograph some pirate routines with an illusion act that we sometimes worked with, leading up to a showcase piece for November. She liked the idea of promoting a whole pirate show to the holiday centres, and we enjoyed being noisy, lively pirates anyway, so we started coming up with some choreography to the illusionist's tracks, ready for November.

I was feeling a lot better in myself at this point, but I still had some moments of anxiety. During these, I often felt overwhelmed or agonised that I wasn't good enough. I'd had a couple of scary experiences in Stratford-upon-Avon, tiny things had set me off crying and shaking. For example, someone cut in front of me at a junction and, instead of swearing under my breath like normal, I found myself unable to breathe and had to pull over, cry and try to comfort myself. In the end, I spoke to my GP about it, and he told me he thought I was having panic attacks. He prescribed a drug called Propranolol, that he told me I could take if I felt panic coming on, because it would stop it very quickly. I carried the tablets around in my bag at all times. If I panicked, I wouldn't always think straight at first, but if I did then remember to take them they seemed to do the trick.

The other thing that seemed to help my mental health was becoming a vegan. Although it pains me to think of it now, I'd always been the type to mock vegans. I was vegetarian and loved animals, but I wasn't very clued up when it came to animal cruelty or farming practices. There were a couple of vegans who worked at the Mare and Foal Sanctuary but they always looked thin and unhealthy, and I wondered why they wouldn't eat dairy or eggs if no animals were killed in these processes. In 2015, I began to understand a lot more, especially after I watched Erin Janus' Youtube video 'Dairy is Scary', which sickened me, and some documentaries on Netflix – 'Cowspiracy' and 'What the Health'. I couldn't believe it: all this time I thought I was doing my best for the animals, but actually I was still contributing to their torture, rape and death.

I didn't become vegan overnight. In 2015, it was still relatively difficult to find alternatives to cheese and eggs, and I wasn't the best cook. I started by switching my milk over to a plant-based alternative, then cut out cheese at home. The hardest thing for me was eggs, as my hangover cure for years had been eggy bread. I eventually stopped eating them in September 2015, when I cracked an egg into a pan, looked at it and suddenly thought, "Ewww, a chicken period!"

The only time I ate dairy or eggs after that was on holiday in Gran Canaria in November 2015, but this was more due to necessity: they barely had vegetarian options, let alone vegan ones. I caved in and ate some dairy throughout the week. However by the time my 30th birthday came around in December 2015 I was fully-vegan and feeling better than ever. My new diet felt more authentically aligned with my beliefs and as an added bonus, I had lost half a stone. I started cooking healthier meals – experimenting with different vegetables and seasoning, and I ate things I'd never really liked before, like bananas. I didn't want to be an unhealthy vegan, as I wanted to be a good role model for others. I encouraged others to try vegan foods and watch the documentaries I'd seen, then I talked to them about living a more peaceful way of life.

However, I had to accept that people needed to come to this realisation in their own time. I must have been quite convincing though: since then, Mum and many of my close friends have become vegan, which makes my life easier. There is so much more information out there now, and there are ever more products available to buy. Nowadays, if I go to a cafe or restaurant and there's not a vegan option, I'm very surprised.

The following year, I attended a meeting with some other vegans in Torbay who were passionate about animal rights. From this gathering, DAS (Devon Animal Save) was born. The Save Movement exists to rescue animals from going to slaughter, or at least to give them respect and recognition in the last moments of their lives before they are killed. We set up some peaceful vigils at slaughterhouses across the South West, to which we invited other vegans and animal lovers to attend via the DAS social media pages. We also set up regular educational stalls in local town centres, where we would give out leaflets and food samples, then talk to people about changing their eating habits. This was quite successful – most people were at least respectful and open to listening. Sometimes, they took away leaflets containing recipes and went straight to Holland & Barrett to find the products we'd been promoting. Of course, sometimes we met farmers and people who opposed what we were doing, or those who just wanted to have an argument. In the end though, we all became very good at pre-empting the objections people would have, countering in a gentle manner. I loved the stalls, because I was so passionate about educating people who, like me, may not have realised the harm they had caused through consuming dairy, eggs and honey, or by using products tested on animals. In addition to volunteering with DAS, I also became an Animal Aid school speaker volunteer so that I could educate children in schools about animals and veganism. In primary schools, talks are mainly aimed at teaching children to respect animals and explaining the purpose of sanctuaries and rescues. In secondary schools and colleges I talked about the ethics of veganism. These presentations can also be tailored to specific subjects, such as the fur trade, dairy industry, hunting, and so on.

As part of my 30th and Mum's 60th birthday celebrations, we booked a holiday to India in March 2016. We were both eager to explore the country that had given us all the fun of Bollywood dance. We did a 'golden triangle' tour, first visiting the hustle and bustle of New Delhi. I've never seen traffic like it – beeping horns and persistent pedlars backed up for miles. Sometimes a motorist would get impatient and simply overtake on the pavement without thinking about the pedestrians. The only time drivers had any consideration was if there was a cow in the road. We went on a rickshaw ride there, the most surprising aspect of which was that we actually survived it after going at such a fast pace down tiny lanes with dreadful road surfacing. Delhi also has a vast array of smells, from fragrant spices to the downright dodgy drainage.

From Delhi we moved on to Agra, home of the famous Taj Mahal. It took our breath away. I could have stayed in the grounds all day, it was so beautiful, but the peace was disturbed by Indian tourists wanting their photographs taken with us. It felt like we were celebrities, but apparently this is quite normal in India.

My favourite place on the tour was Ranthambore. Here, life seemed a lot more relaxed compared to the crazy cities, and our hotel was beautiful, with an outdoor swimming pool and cocktail bar. It felt like paradise after the dusty, noisy streets of Delhi. Here, we went on a morning and afternoon jeep safari and were lucky enough to see a tiger on our second trip. She strolled by, incredibly close to the jeep, looking magnificent. The tour guide told us she was the mother tiger, who lived in the park with her two sons. I was excited after seeing her, but I was hungry for more, so I asked what the odds were of us seeing a jackal. The guide laughed and told me that they are rarely sighted, but just a few minutes later one appeared. The guide told me I was the tour's good luck charm. Although we did not see the sloth bear, which was next on my list, the tour was packed with glimpses of countless other native animals.

Our final destination was Jaipur, the pink city. It was still very busy in town, but there were lots of lovely temples and sights to see, and I particularly enjoyed the colourful markets there. I bought some salwar kameez, traditional Indian dress that Becky and I later wore to dance in at the 'Bollywood nights' back in the UK. I also saw a cow helping itself to items from a food stall.

We visited at the time of Holi, the spring festival of colours. During the celebrations everyone throws brightly coloured paints around and parties throughout the day and night. We wore white sheet gowns, which were covered in paint by the end of the day, and traditional hats. We didn't hold back, getting involved in all the fun: Mum and I even ended up Bollywood dancing on a stage at someone's party!

But, there were sad undertones in India. The way women are treated in some places is horrifying. At the hotel in Agra, a city teeming with tourists, the staff wouldn't speak to us or acknowledge us because of our gender. Our guide admitted to having more than one wife and said that it was still common. I once asked him what a billboard, which showed a picture of a child crying, was alluding to. To my surprise, he told me the wording translated to 'Save the girl child': the government wanted to deter people from committing infanticide. Many families can't afford additional children and want a male heir, so it is quite common to kill female children in secret until a male arrives, a problem made worse by the lack of widely available contraception in India. We saw many beggars at the side of the road, often without limbs, and our guide would explain that they may even have chopped them off themselves to extract donations for sympathy. I came away from India with lovely memories, but a sense of sadness and despair at how cruel the world can be.

During the showcase in November 2015, we had featured a taste of our Pirate Adventure show. From this we were booked to perform at a couple of different holiday centres the following summer. We continued with our own 'So Street' and 'Dynamique' shows too, but the pirate act gave us some variety and it was nice to work with the illusionists. Everything was busy and exciting and we enjoyed ourselves.

The following year, we were booked to The Tor Park Hotel instead of The Esplanade to give any repeat customers a break from us. Entertainments budgets were being slashed everywhere, which meant that I was asked to host the night as well as perform. I agreed, as we were keen to get the work, but it didn't work out well. There was no one to introduce the show and create a build up, as I had to run off to get changed before the performance. My double role also meant that there was no one to take us off at the end and encourage applause. I found it challenging, and the guests obviously didn't approve either. Mum received some complaints from the hotel, who said that our show wasn't up to scratch and asked if we could be pulled out. It was a big knock to our confidence to hear this, and while I told the girls and myself that the absence of a host was the cause, it still hurt. As a result, we had lost a large chunk of work for the year.

Mum spoke to me and asked if I might consider hosting at the hotel for another act, or even setting up a duo with my friend Karma, who also sang and danced. I'd known her for ages, having appeared with her in the 'Around the World' show all those years ago.

Karma and I had stayed in touch, and she'd recently been encouraging me to sing again. She said that I had a great voice for singing pop songs, which dovetailed well with her plans to create a three-piece tribute to some famous girl bands. This would include tracks by the Spice Girls, Sugababes, Little Mix, the Supremes and more. At first I'd been very reluctant, as I hadn't sung since my break down and felt it opened me up to too much criticism. However, with her encouragement, I eventually decided I'd get together with her and another girl, Luisa, to see what we sounded like. Not long after, 'Sugar Rush' was born. We promoted ourselves for the summer season that year and ended up doing three great shows, but sadly the budget wasn't there for a trio in the majority of the venues.

Karma was excited at the thought of performing with me as a duo at The Tor Park, but I still hadn't quite found my confidence. For the first couple of shows, she performed on her own while I did the sound and lights and hosted the evening. However, we rehearsed some songs together and I started feeling more comfortable. Karma encouraged me to put in a tap routine to one of the songs she sang, and made up some routines to 'Cabaret' and an Andrews Sisters medley that we could perform. Within a couple of months, I was fully embracing the mix of vocals and dance and enjoying singing again. It helped that Karma was on stage with me; I knew that if I wasn't feeling up to it, I could dip out and she would do the show solo. We bounced off each other really well on stage – I became the comedy character while she stayed sensible and straight. The audience loved the different dynamics we brought to the show.

In 2018, we were booked back to The Tor Park and The Esplanade as a duo. We simply called ourselves 'Ami and Karma'. Around this time, encouraged by Karma and my singing teacher, Lisa, I decided to showcase myself as a solo vocalist again and take some gigs on my own. I built up slowly, starting with smaller venues in the local area. I enjoyed them, because I was starting to see what counted: seeing singing as a hobby rather than as a career meant I could relax, and it freed me from worrying about what people thought about me. Mum had sold the agency by this point, as she wanted to slow down before her retirement, and I also felt that working for different agents relieved the pressure I had felt to do well for her. She had asked me if I felt I'd like to take the agency on at some point, as she had from her parents. I refused. Seeing her work such long days, under so much stress, had put me off it completely.

Around this time, Cilla's epilepsy had started getting worse. She was having seizures at least monthly now, sometimes even weekly, and we'd upped her dosage of epilepsy medications again. One day, I took her for a routine vaccination at the vets and she had her first cluster seizure when we arrived home. I gave her two vials of the rectal valium, but it didn't make her stop, so I called upon my neighbour to rush us back to the vets. Eventually, they got her onto a drip to help stabilise her. Following this incident, Mum and I took Cilla to Cave Veterinary Specialists again to try and find out what was happening. They gave her an MRI scan and spinal tap, but still could only tell us that it was idiopathic epilepsy and it was likely that she needed to try a new drug. We gave it a try; I'd have tried anything for her. In the meantime, I turned to some canine epilepsy support groups on Facebook for help and advice. A lady called Lucy, who I'd corresponded with before, recommended trying a holistic vet. I thought this sounded ridiculous, after all, if the specialist vets to whom we'd already paid thousands of pounds couldn't find an answer, how would this man? Still, it was worth a shot, so I found myself taking Cilla all the way to Oxford to visit Christopher Day. Chris explained to me that, according to his research, only about ten percent of dogs diagnosed with epilepsy actually have true epilepsy; the other 90 percent have sensitivity to chemicals or stress. He put Cilla on his examination table and we both watched her go rigid; she was stressed at being touched by a stranger. He gave me two homeopathic remedies; one for stress and one to help her detox from chemicals. He also advised me to stop vaccinating her, switch her flea and worm treatments to herbal remedies, swap household cleaners for vinegar, lemon and water and feed her a raw meat and vegetable diet.

"I can't feed her a raw diet, I'm vegan. I literally can't think of anything worse," I told him.

"I understand, I'm vegetarian," he replied. "You can buy frozen, raw food in ready cut pieces. You defrost it overnight and put it down for her to eat in the morning. You won't have to touch it at all."

I was still unsure, but when we got back to Torquay the next day, I bought some and started the weaning process from her old food to the new regime.

A month passed and Cilla didn't have any seizures. Then two months, then three, and when we got to a year, I was convinced that Chris Day was a miracle worker. Why hadn't any of the previous vets ever told me these simple things that would save my dog from suffering? Every dog is individual and epilepsy affects them all differently, as do the treatments. However, surely the things Chris had told me were the starting point for treatment, rather than rushing straight to medicating with tablets.

I talked to my friend Abbie from Devon Animal Save about Cilla and she was really interested. Abbie is a keen documentary maker and animal lover, so I was delighted when she asked whether she could make a 'dogumentary' about Cilla and her journey with epilepsy. I thought that if we could help other dogs and owners who were going through what we had, then that would be really positive. Filming took a few months, and we interviewed other companions of epileptic dogs to get some different views and experiences. Mum voiced Cilla, bringing her to life with a fun personality. When it was finished, the 'dogumentary' was fantastic. It was educational, interesting, fun and gave a positive message for other dog owners out there. Abbie uploaded the finished article to YouTube and we both shared it on several canine forums online.

In June 2017, I finished the final exam for my Open University degree. It had taken me ten years on and off, but I'd persevered and finally got it done. I tried not to think about how it had gone; I told myself I'd given it my best shot while working several different jobs and battling with my mental health. To my delight, I eventually got a letter to say I'd gained a 2:1 BA degree in Psychology and Philosophy, and I graduated in October 2017. There was a lovely ceremony, with Mum and Grandad watching on proudly, followed by a party at a local vegan restaurant with close friends and family.

As I'd found out my results prior to my graduation, I had already started looking around for new job roles by this time. Although I was happy at the Mare and Foal Sanctuary, I also felt that I had come as far as I could with my journey there. Sumo had passed away in December 2016, and while I didn't feel this was a reason to leave, I also didn't feel like anything was holding me there. I was in no rush to find a new job, but there were some fun opportunities to be found and I would soon be moving on.

Chapter 14 – Under Lock and Key

At 8.30a.m. I moved quickly across the concrete courtyard, looking up at the big, grey Victorian buildings surrounding me. Even from outside it was noisy – shouting, metal doors clanging, alarms sounding. A lazy cat sat on the grass verge, employed to catch rats around the buildings, and there were plenty of them too. I retrieved my keys from my belt and swiftly opened the gate, then pulled it shut and quickly locked it behind me.

"Morning Miss," said a smiling man with a bald head and twinkling eyes, who sat on the bottom step by the gate. Every morning he was eager to get to his work and loved the routine. He said it made the days pass quicker. Sometimes I'd stop to chat, but on other mornings I was in a hurry to get down to my office in the cellar of D wing. Why was I in prison? Another new job: I'd been working in the Substance Misuse department at HMP Exeter for seven months as an administrative assistant. This week I was interviewing for a support worker role and was keen to go over some questions with my supportive colleagues to help me prepare.

Upon obtaining the results of my degree, I had applied for this role and for a receptionist position at CAMHS (Children and Adolescent Mental Health Services). I'd had my heart set on the latter, and although I interviewed well, I was told I missed out because another candidate had more relevant experience. However, my new manager told me I'd been selected for the role at HMP Exeter the day after I'd interviewed, and they were eager for me to start. It took considerable time for my enhanced DBS (disclosure and barring) check and prison vetting process to be completed – so long in fact, that after three months, they let me start my new job regardless as the workload in the department was backing up. However, I wasn't allowed my gate keys until confirmation finally came through, which meant I was mainly confined to the office. A prison within a prison. This suited me fine though; although I loved the new environment and found the work incredibly interesting, working in an all-male prison felt extremely intimidating at first. On my way to the office for the first few months I kept my head down and tried not to make eye contact with anyone, just in case. Mum had fuelled my fear, making it obvious that she was worried about me going into work there with such dangerous people. I was curious throughout though, wanting to know about the different courses that were being run, how different medications worked to help people with substance withdrawal, and why prisoners often returned to jail as if they owned timeshares there.

Exeter is a remand prison, which means that in some cases men stay for just a couple of days before being released. In others, they may spend a short sentence at Exeter, while long-stay prisoners may spend the first part of their sentence there before moving on to a different establishment. It's a Category B prison, but because it is remand, a lot of the prisoners are just held there until they can be recategorised and moved to a Cat C or D, which is lower security. In my time there, we also had a couple of Cat A prisoners, who were taken straight into the segregation unit and held until a space became available at a more suitable establishment. I knew pretty much nothing about the prison system until I started working there, so it was a whole new education for me. After a few months I finally got my keys. I became less nervous and started speaking with some of the men who were on D wing when I arrived at work or left for the day. As D wing was the enhanced wing, the men housed there had gained their place due to good behaviour. To me, they seemed less scary than the prisoners on the main wings. I'd only set foot on the noisier A, B and C wings a couple of times, and had always gone there with colleagues.

That was until curiosity got the better of me. In a supervision session one week, I asked my manager if I would be able to shadow some of the recovery workers and support workers in the substance misuse groups. The team mainly ran SMART (Self Management and Recovery Training) meetings. These were either run as eight to ten-week guided courses with different topics to work on each week alongside a workbook, or as a mutual-aid meeting for clients to talk freely about the difficulties they'd experienced on their road to recovery. My manager agreed, so I accompanied two recovery workers to my first meeting. There were six clients in the group that day, and I remember thinking how laid back and normal they all seemed. They said hello to me when I was introduced, then sat around drinking coffee and vaping. Some of them had great input and insight, while others sat and quietly took in what was being said. It wasn't just for model students: one attendee smirked and yawned throughout and wanted to leave halfway through. Generally though, it was considered to be a good group. I suddenly realised that actually, obviously, these were just people. People who had been through difficult times and felt they had to resort to petty crimes and drugs, people with mental health and addiction challenges, people who had just taken the wrong path in life. As I asked questions after the group and learned about the men's lives and how they'd ended up there, I felt real compassion towards some of them. Of course, there were also dangerous, manipulative men within the prison, so we never let our guard down. Despite this, I found most of the people I encountered to be pleasant, polite and grateful for support.

I attended another couple of groups and took more opportunities to accompany my support worker colleagues onto the landings, just so I could take it all in. I felt really privileged to be in an environment that not many people are able to experience and to be privy to some of the conversations the men had with the prison staff. I realised I wanted to help them, which was when I decided I would interview for the support worker role.

The administration manager was upset, as she'd found me to be quick and efficient in my role, but she also understood. The real reason I'd gone for the job was because I wanted to use my skills and my degree, so I was testing the water to see if I could work in this environment.

My interview went well, and straight after I took my mind off things by going shopping for a new car with a friend of Dad's. The brakes on my old one had failed when I was on my friend Lisa's drive a few weeks earlier. Luckily for me, Lisa and her husband had a car each and could survive with just the one, so I'd broken down in the right place at the right time. I'd stayed overnight at her house, had my car towed away the next day, then test drove and loved her 4 x 4. I wanted to keep that car, but I found the most gorgeous MG ZS while looking that day – still high off the ground which was important for me, but in my price range. While speaking to the car dealer, my phone rang and I excused myself. It was Cat, one of the recovery workers who'd interviewed me with one of the service managers.

"How do you think you did today, Ami?"

"Well, I think I was able to answer the questions, but whether I said the right things is another matter. Perhaps I should have..."

"You did great!" she said cutting me off. "I'm calling to tell you you've got the job!"

I started laughing happily, "You scared me there."

"Oh, you should have heard yourself," she giggled.

I went to bed happy that night, with a new job and a new car.

Back at work the next day, I was told I needed to work my notice in the administration role for a couple of months until they found someone to take my place. I fully understood, but knowing I would be transitioning into my new role, I started asking more questions, reading the SMART manuals and shadowing wherever possible. One of my favourite people to shadow was the prescriber, Jamie. He had seen a lot in his career, both inside and outside of the prison, and spoke to the men in a firm but fair way. He had a lot of empathy with them too. I remember him taking the history of a man in his thirties, who had been in and out of prison over 20 times.

The man was quiet, but when he spoke it was obvious he just felt he had no one to turn to and no other options in life besides drugs and crime. When he left the room, Jamie and I both had tears in our eyes. Of course, men would also come to him demanding higher doses of methadone because they felt desperately ill, but he would examine them, and if they weren't showing signs of withdrawal, he would ask them to wait it out a little longer. They didn't always like this, but Jamie would tell them he was happy to see them again in a couple of days if they didn't feel better.

It took a few months to get someone new into the admin post, after advertising, interviews, vetting and checks, so even after I moved into my support worker role, I was asked to do one day a week in the administration office with my colleague Sheena. I felt this was fair, but Sheena wasn't so keen. When I first started working with the loud, outspoken Sheena, I was again intimidated. She made it clear that she wanted to get on with her role without having to train me, and she would also make it obvious to the men in the groups that she was in charge, talking over me or disagreeing with things I said. Eventually, I decided I'd talk to her and try to get to know her better as we had to work as a team, which was a good idea. She hadn't even realised that she had been so intimidating, but we could both laugh at it and from then on we became firm friends. We loved running groups together: I'd take a softer approach, while Sheena would tell it like it was. I learnt a lot from her no-nonsense, straight-talking attitude.

My manager, Emma, asked me one day if I'd be interested in organising a new project. She knew that I was creative, as a dancer and entertainer, and wondered how I felt about helping to run a creative writing course? Of course, I was extremely interested. I'd written songs since I was a little girl, and during my own mental health challenges, I had developed a great belief in the power of journaling. I thought it could be a good release for some of our clients. Emma had a contact called Pippa, a writer who had volunteered to deliver the course, and we decided that we'd trial it in the week leading up to Christmas 2018. Pippa and I exchanged emails about how it would be run, then I spoke to recovery workers to see if any of the clients on their caseloads would be interested in attending. A few names were put forward, but there was still some room on the list. I thought back to the quiet young man Jamie and I had spoken to; I'd remembered him saying he played guitar and wrote music. I found him on the landings and explained what we were doing. He was painfully shy and seemed unsure, but he agreed to sign up. Sheena was also excited about the project and suggested a couple of the clients from the SMART groups. By the time we came to launching the group, we had ten names on our list. Six of the men showed up to the sessions, which was over half – in our eyes this was an achievement.

Pippa chose different topics for the prisoners to write about. She realised that Christmas may be a difficult time for some, as they were away from families and in some cases their children, so gave them prompts to articulate this. The standard of writing didn't matter: many prisoners are unable to read or write well, and a lot are dyslexic. We would play games to get them thinking about words or sentences. If they struggled, we would assist them in getting their words on to paper. Generally, the group was run by Pippa, me and one other member of the team, so there were enough of us to assist with the writing. One of the men was from outside of the UK and only had a basic grasp of English, but he wrote and benefitted from the course too. At the end of the week, the men presented their work to the rest of the Substance Misuse staff. We had two songs, a story and some poems. Everyone was really impressed, and it was agreed that for 2019 we would run a weekly session. This was generally run by Pippa, but if she was unable to attend, Sheena and I would come up with some fun ideas too.

The creative writing group was therapeutic for the prisoners, but also for me, as I enjoyed pushing myself to write about different topics and opening up in front of a group of people. All of the participants were very supportive of each other. This was one of the rules of the course, and it was always respected. It was sometimes strange to see a man, who would be out on the landings acting like he owned the place throughout the week, come into the group on a Monday and express himself, sometimes even shedding a tear. It showed me just how powerful writing is.

I worked at HMP Exeter three days per week. Mondays were usually group day for me; I would be present for the creative writing course in the mornings, then SMART in the afternoons. On Tuesdays I had a 'duty' day, which meant I would be asked to complete any urgent tasks within the department. This normally involved the initial assessments of anyone who had been referred to us, and talking to new prisoners who had just arrived about whether they'd like to be referred to our service. If they were already on a methadone script or alcohol detox, they'd automatically be referred. Most weren't keen at first, as they'd just arrived and wanted to process what was going on, but a lot of them would get back to us later on and ask for help. I also might have been asked to speak to anyone who had taken NPS (known as 'Spice'), a drug rife in prisons. It often caused the men to foam at the mouth, to lose the ability to speak properly, have seizures or pass out. Someone from our team would visit them the next day to try and find out why they were using, ask if we could give them any support, and remind them of the dangers of this drug. Especially in prison, 'Spice' can be mixed with all manner of things - rat poison, car cleaner, etc - to make it look like you get more for your money. I found duty days really interesting, and I got a lot more used to speaking to the men and listening to their stories. On Fridays, I would usually run a group or catch up on my admin, then help with duty tasks, attend our team meeting and give out invitations to the Monday groups.

HMP Exeter also has a prison band. One of the men from the creative writing group attended every Monday, and when I found out about it I went along to see what they were up to. The band was run by a professional musician called Dave, who worked for a charity called 'Changing Tunes'. He taught people how to play, or encouraged those who already could. The men suggested songs to perform, or could present their original material to the rest of the group, which they'd then arrange accompaniment to. I was really inspired by the talent I saw. One of the men, the drummer, I even recognised from a well-known band in Torbay and I felt quite star struck. Somehow, it got out that I could sing and a couple of the men were eager to have my input while they played. I've always wanted to front a rock band, so I was excited to have this opportunity. Dave and I talked through some options and decided on 'Weak' by Skunk Anansie and 'Zombie' by the Cranberries. The band learned the tracks, then I'd go and belt them out on Mondays after my groups had finished.

Working with people with genuine substance issues was incredibly eye-opening. I learned about several new drugs that I never knew existed, such as Krokodil, a derivative of codeine mixed with other chemicals. The side effects are awful and can include skin ulcerations, gangrene, and cause people to need limb amputations. One man showed me the scars from his injections, and it looked like his flesh had been eaten away. I also heard a few stories about men taking Valium, a prescription drug used to relieve anxiety and relax muscles. They couldn't remember anything after taking large quantities of this: they'd just wake up in a police cell and be told they'd done all sorts of things that were out of character for them. One man had run into a kebab shop, grabbed a knife from behind the counter and started wielding it at customers. He reportedly remembered nothing about this. Some of the scariest stories I heard came from alcohol use. Alcohol is the number one killer drug in the UK, and yet it is legal. People have a few too many drinks, then act out of character or spiral out of control with disastrous consequences. A man broke down in a group, having been charged with manslaughter after a drunken fight.

He couldn't remember much of the night, but apparently his opponent had hit his head hard on the pavement and died from his injuries. It made me think about how many people I knew who had been in fights under the influence of alcohol. They could have easily been in this position. Another man told me that although he couldn't remember exactly what happened, he'd cut off another man's thumb with a knife in front of his children while he was drunk.

I started thinking seriously about my own drinking. I had been a big drinker when I was in show business, and it had been a part of my life for such a long time. Drinking was expected at family parties, weddings, or even just at the weekends. I always had a couple of bottles of wine in the house 'in case I had a bad day' or 'if my back was bad' or 'if I wanted to celebrate'. I also thought about the effects it had on me – I've blacked out several times while drunk, and I've done some of the most ridiculous things: text messages I've regretted, flashing my knickers on a night out, falling asleep in taxis. I'd recently lost my phone, purse and house keys on a night out, but luckily I had friends with me who had taken me home. I'd had paramedics called out after I'd been so sick from drinking too much. When I looked at my drinking history, it wasn't pretty, and I had to admit that the bad outweighed the good. I didn't want to be a laughing stock due to alcohol. I worried about what the effects were on Cilla too: if she had a seizure and I was fast asleep under the influence of alcohol, I wouldn't wake up. I don't think this has ever happened, but I also can't be sure. In May 2019, I decided to give drinking a rest. I've never said "I'll never drink again", because I wouldn't want to put that pressure on myself, but I actually enjoy weddings and events more now. I like to have clarity around what's going on and remember things. I also don't have to worry about hangovers or spending too much, because I'm totally in control. I prefer sobriety, and I'm really proud of it. It's one of the best things that came out of working at HMP Exeter.

By the summer, changes were happening within the department. Our managers told us that our contracts would be updated to include weekend service imminently. It was also difficult to see where I could progress within the service: recovery worker positions had to be full-time, and as much as I loved the job, I wasn't ready to give up my dance classes to do this yet. I was still teaching on Wednesdays at local schools, running a summer cheerleading course for language students and teaching children on the weekends at a dance studio. Plus, I was still working with Karma in the hotels, singing on Wednesday and Friday evenings. I was busy and I loved the variety.

I encountered some of the most genuine people I've ever met working at HMP Exeter, people who really want to affect change and help others; friends who I'll hopefully keep for life. Looking back, I'm so glad I got that job, but circumstances meant the time had come to start looking for some new opportunities.

Chapter 15 – Changing Times

My friend Zoe had been working as a social worker for children's services for a few years with a local council. She told me regularly that I'd be a great asset working on their teams as a family practitioner, and while I didn't think I had the skills or experience for it, Zoe persuaded me that I had transferable skills.

Things always seem to turn up at the right time for me. I guess that's how the universe works – you trust and it answers. For this reason I was not too surprised that soon after I decided to leave the prison, Zoe got in touch to let me know about a family practitioner post that was being advertised.

"The deadline is Monday, so you need to get cracking," she told me. It was Thursday. I had work on Friday, followed by a Bollywood class in the evening, classes throughout the day on Saturday and a gig that evening too. Family commitments blocked the day on Sunday. It didn't leave me much time.

"There's always a lot of interest, which is why we put a short deadline on it. We'd be overwhelmed with applications otherwise," Zoe told me.

"Is it a waste of my time doing this?" I asked.

Zoe reassured me that she wouldn't have suggested going for the job if she didn't think I'd be in with a chance. However, because she was on the interview panel, she couldn't help with my application. Despite this, she was able to offer some good general advice. First was the importance of transferable skills.

"All your skills are transferable, so when you write your personal statement, bear that in mind. You have a lot of experience with children as a dance teacher, and you've carried out assessments on your clients in the prison. A lot of those clients have children and you may have had to advise on that."

This was true. Not long previously, I had needed to research the adoption process to help one of my clients gain an understanding of it.

"Exactly," continued Zoe. "It's things like that which will show you have the skills and knowledge. Also some of the parents and children you'd be working with may be affected by substance misuse or domestic violence, which you know about. You'll be fine. Get writing your application!"

I settled down to work on Sunday evening, after an early dinner. I was awake reading the criteria and typing madly until 1a.m., when I finally emailed it over. All I had to do was wait and see if I would be chosen for the interview.

Zoe called me a few days later to give me the good news. "I've just emailed an invite to an interview Tuesday week. Can you make it?"

I was delighted, and it was also agreed that Zoe could stay on the panel, as I wasn't interviewing for her team directly. I had applied to a different team because of the part-time hours. There were three positions going, and this was the only one that would fit around my dance business.

Interview day came around quickly. I'd been practicing possible questions and reading up as much as I could about the organisation and the role. Then I pulled into the big council offices car park alongside a dead hedgehog. Not a good start. I had to not let it upset me and get into the building without looking at it. I was greeted at reception by a short, smiling lady who, after introductions, took me into a room with a desk with some instructions and paper on it. She said she'd be back in 15 minutes.

Zoe hadn't told me about this part of the interview. The paper described some scenarios and asked what I would do if faced with each one. I outlined several points, then wrote about the services I'd be looking to signpost to. I wrote a lot in those 15 minutes, and I could have gone on for longer, but the small, bespectacled woman came back and told me it was time to follow her upstairs for the interview.

Zoe smiled at me as I walked into the room and sat down. Next to her was another smiling lady, who introduced herself as the manager for the position I was interviewing for. I was told they would ask a few questions each. Zoe poured some water for me, and I breathed, trying to calm myself and think philosophically. Whatever happens, happens.

I can't remember the questions they asked, but I remember talking a lot and being able to read Zoe's facial expressions: she'd tell me subconsciously if I'd said the right things, or if they wanted to hear more. Afterwards she told me she'd tried her hardest to keep a poker face, but when you've known someone for 30 years, you know their expressions. I left feeling that I'd done my best and drove to Grandad's for a catch up. As I got through his door, my phone beeped; a message from Zoe to say I had done well.

I got a call the next day from the manager, offering me the job. I accepted instantly, and she emailed over the formalities. Then, I called Zoe to thank her for her help. She was characteristically modest.

"Well, I didn't really help you, as I wasn't allowed. You were amazing on your own, and I'm not being biased. One lady had more experience, but she wanted a full-time position, so we've been able to take her on in the other team."

The next week I handed in my notice at the prison. I was sad to be leaving, but as my notice period was two months, I had a good amount of time to continue my work and say my goodbyes. I decided not to let any of my clients know until my final week, so as not to unsettle them. My managers were brilliant – they asked if there was still anything I wanted to do in the job that I'd not yet got around to before I left, and they continued to give me training opportunities until the end. Sheena was sad that I was going, but we made sure we spent lots of time together in our lunch breaks and after work, and I promised that I'd keep in touch.

My last week was emotional. Out of all my jobs it was probably the hardest to leave, as I still felt I had a lot to learn. I enjoyed the experience and I was eager to know what would happen to the clients with whom I had built up a good rapport. Sheena said that she would update me, but it still wasn't the same. Strangely, I would miss the noise and the smells too; everything about this unique atmosphere.

My last day was a Monday, so I could attend the creative writing group. All of the regular clients had, prompted by Pippa, written a poem or note for me and attached it to a rose to make a bunch of well wishes. I had to try my hardest to keep the tears at bay. The substance misuse team held a farewell vegan lunch for me, and they also took the time to write haikus and positive messages for me, which I put into a jar to keep and read from time to time. Again, I was on the verge of tears. On the Monday afternoon, I completed my final SMART group with Sheena and said goodbye to the clients I'd got to know there. I then went up to the chapel to say goodbye to the band members, but when I reached it, only Dave was left.

"You're too late, we had to finish early today because of the altered regime."

"Oh no!" I exclaimed, and finally the tears came. I would miss the band so much, and I'd not even got a chance to say goodbye. I was comforted by Dave and we exchanged numbers, as he also ran various bands on the outside. He said I may be able to get involved with these at some point. I ran around the landings madly to try and locate the band members and say goodbye, then returned to the office and cleared my desk. Sheena gave me a big hug and I cried some more.

"I don't want to leave..."

"Then don't." She made it sound so simple.

Cilla had stayed with a friend in Exeter all day, so I collected her after work. We drove up to the New Forest, where I'd booked a log cabin to stay in and relax for the remainder of the week, the perfect rest before starting my new job the next week. It was a lovely break and gave me time to reflect on my time in HMP Exeter and read through all my notes again.

Including my own:

It's a little nerve-wracking when you step out of what you know, out of your comfort zone, beyond feeling safe in a little world of friends, routine and normality (whatever your normal is). You go out into the big bad world, become the new girl again, learn new things and meet new people.

The change in me, thanks to this experience, has been massive. I was quiet and timid when I started. I sat at my desk and hardly moved throughout the day. The noise put me off going out of my office. I was scared. Then, I realised, I could do more. I wanted to make a difference.

At first, holding someone's hand, I'd go and move around, meet people and experience everything. I built up confidence, I learned, and soon I was happy to start conversations, lead groups, laugh and wander around. There's no going back now. Certain people here have helped to shape the new me. I thank you.

I will not say goodbye, for I will always carry parts of you with me in my heart and in my mind forever. You will be with me every step of the way in my new ventures. I won't go back to who I was. I won't be scared. I'll think of you and know I can pull up my big girl pants and rock it!

I began my new job the following Monday. To start with, I hated it. There was no real induction and no one to train me. Occasionally, I'd be able to shadow someone, but I felt totally lost. For the first few weeks, I had no clients and I was bored.

My colleagues told me to enjoy this while it lasted. Apparently I'd be very busy soon. However, I missed the crazy prison environment and the noise. I never had a minute to myself there, as someone would get my attention, wanting to talk about their methadone script, their course, or just because they wanted a chat.

Soon, there were a few families assigned to me, and I would go to their houses or take children out and do what I thought was right, but I got no feedback or help with it apart from intermittent supervisions. However, the families I worked with liked me and I seemed to be helping them, which was my main reason for doing the job, so I persevered. I enjoyed having conversations with people from a variety of backgrounds, carrying out parenting assessments that delved into their lives. I tried to find out more and put the pieces together.

I was learning a big lesson; sometimes you have to find your own way and use your initiative, rather than having someone hold your hand throughout. I had been trusted to do this job well, I had the skills. I just needed more confidence, which would come in time.

Then came March 2020, and the Covid-19 pandemic sent us into a national lockdown. My job was safe, as the work still needed to be carried out, but I was unable to teach or sing. Grandad had been in hospital with heart problems for six weeks prior to lockdown, and he was discharged on the day restrictions were announced. Mum went into a panic. He would need looking after, but she didn't want other people entering the house for fear of him contracting the virus. Between us, we decided that we'd both move into Grandad's house for a couple of weeks to help him get back on his feet. This way, Mum could help him with any personal care needs (which I'd point blank refused to do) and I could do any lifting that was required, which she was unable to do with her bad back.

I told work that I'd be unable to do face-to-face visits, as I needed to shield for my Grandad, but I could carry out virtual visits and work from home. At the time I had a temporary manager who said that she didn't think this was acceptable, which caused me some stress, but when my manager (who had been off sick herself with Covid-19) returned, she was a lot more sympathetic. She told me to let her know what I needed, and checked that my workload was manageable. I was very productive in this time, and kept in regular contact with all my clients. I got the work done, despite having Grandad intermittently shouting for cups of tea.

Grandad was more poorly than we'd realised. Although he had returned home, he was still catheterised, which neither Mum nor I had any experience of. He had some supplies and medication, but not enough to keep him going for more than a few days, and at this time, trying to get hold of a doctor was near impossible. Mum spent much of her time on the phone as I googled how to change catheters. Mum wasn't keen on the district nurses attending the house, because they'd been carrying out visits to other people, but she realised it was necessary in this situation and I assured her that they would wear PPE and be extremely careful. They were able to demonstrate some of his care for us and gave us a number that we could call in an emergency.

In total, Mum and I stayed in Grandad's tiny bungalow with him for six weeks straight. I shared a bed with her and Cilla, and most of the time we were pretty happy. We had great weather, so we'd sit in the garden and chat, we'd go for short walks with Cilla, and we'd cook lovely nutritious meals together. We started filming some dance classes in the garden to put online for our students, which Grandad watched and tried to join in a little from the conservatory window. He also found this very amusing. In the evenings we'd watch films, 'Strictly Come Dancing' DVDs, or comedy classics like 'Fawlty Towers'. Grandad was happy to tell his stories to us. Many of these we'd heard several times over, or even been present for, but it kept him animated and enthusiastic.

I took up mindfulness and meditation during this time. My friend Danielle had sent me some links to Deepak Chopra's meditations just before lockdown started, and I listened to these with Mum at night before bed. Shalini, my Just Jhoom! instructor, had also started a mindful meditation group on Zoom, which I joined because I was definitely feeling more relaxed thanks to the ones I'd already been doing. I was apprehensive at first, because I don't like going into groups with people that I don't know. I'm happy to sing or dance in front of hundreds of strangers, but I'm an introvert at heart and, unless I'm with people I know well, I can feel quite intimidated. Before long we were all opening up to each other about how the meditations made us feel, and the ten of us (who took part regularly) became friends.

Most of the time, it was fun living at Grandad's house, but there were also some really hard times too. Grandad was often in pain and we didn't know how to manage it. We'd need to try and get hold of nurses, and whilst we waited, we'd get really upset as we listened to him moan in pain. Mum also got stressed and shouted at him a couple of times, especially when he was being demanding in the middle of the night. Although he was poorly, he was still quite capable of doing a lot for himself, including walking around, but he'd play on us being there and demand more cups of tea, or for us to bring him things while we were in the middle of something. After six weeks, it was decided that we needed a break, and we were lucky enough to find someone who could carry out live-in care for three days a week. I was so happy to get back home; to relax and sleep in my own bed for those three days. It was like a well-deserved holiday.

In August 2020, lockdown restrictions eased somewhat and Mum started to allow social services carers in to see Grandad a few times a day. They would help to get him up, put him to bed and make his lunch. They were more familiar with catheters and medication, so it took a lot of the responsibility away from us. We also found a care agency that could provide a full-time companion for Grandad, so that we could move out as he'd have company all the time.

A couple of days before restrictions lifted, I had a call from an old friend. I'd known Cheryl since I was a child, as she was the main vocalist in the 'Rock Rock Rock' show, but her current project was a Bananarama tribute band. She had been looking for a support vocalist in case one of her trio was unable to perform due to illness, holiday, etc. I applied for the position and Cheryl sent me the dance routines and lyrics, which I learned through lockdown. There was a show scheduled for the first Saturday night after restrictions were lifted, and Cheryl asked me to take part. I was incredibly excited and told her I would. I knew the other members in the band – in fact, one was Karma, who had joined Cheryl about a year before, and I would be doing my first performance with her too. We got together on the Thursday afternoon to go through the routines, then spent the day together on the Saturday before performing locally at Hoburne Torbay Holiday Centre that evening. Due to restrictions, we had to wear masks at all times (when we weren't singing) and we had to perform our set twice as the venue could only allow a certain number of people in the clubhouse at any one time. However, I enjoyed both sets, as I've always been a big fan of 80s music. The dance routines were really fun: I wore some amazing dungarees as part of my costume, and it was lovely to be on stage with Cheryl and Karma again. I forgot some of the lyrics to a song during the second set, but I covered convincingly and Cheryl told me not to beat myself up too much. Instead, I congratulated myself on learning the show and going on stage with just two days' notice.

During the brief period of freedom between August and October, I was also able to go back to teaching dance classes with limited numbers, and I took some of my own solo gigs, started back with face-to-face visits for work, and felt happy to be busy and sociable again.

Another dance teacher, Louise, got in touch with me in September to ask if I'd like to meet up and discuss a business opportunity. Never one to miss out, I arranged to meet her the following week at a local restaurant, where we could get some tasty vegan food. I had assumed that the opportunity would be something to do with dancing, but Louise excitedly told me about an online health and wellness business she'd started during lockdown. This was helping her make some extra income, but also helped her feel amazing. She certainly looked full of vitality, so I took away some information and samples and promptly forgot about it. Louise prompted me a couple of weeks later to ask how I was getting on. 'Oops', I thought, 'better look into this'.

I felt pretty healthy, but knew some of my friends had become deficient in certain vitamins since hitting their 30s. I'd had some blood tests done while I was working at The Mare and Foal Sanctuary, because we were part of a health plan there, and I'd been interested to find out whether turning vegan had affected my body in any way. They'd come back completely fine; but that didn't mean it wasn't sensible to ensure I was getting my full quota of nutrients each day. I was also aware that, although I was pretty clued up on what I needed to eat, I could be sloppy. On busy work days, I sometimes just grabbed a banana for breakfast and crisps for lunch. The health plan Louise was offering came with supplements, online workouts, a tailored nutrition plan and a mindset workbook. I decided I'd give it a go, as I had nothing to lose and possibly a lot to gain. We talked it through and I signed up as her business partner. If it went well for me, and people started asking me about it, I might as well earn some extra cash.

Already in the first week of the health plan, I started feeling more healthy and energetic than I ever had in my life. By the end of the first month I was getting up earlier to embrace the extra hours of the day before work to do a fitness class and read personal development books. My clothes were fitting better and I felt more confident. After two and a half months, I conquered my fear of the scales for the first time in over seven years. With a new, happy mindset, none of it mattered to me anymore: I could accept myself. I had so much gratitude for Louise for introducing me to the first health plan I had ever been able to get on board with, as it educated me about my body and what I needed to feel good. Previously I'd been exposed to a diet culture that fed my body dysmorphia, encouraging me to count calories, no matter what source they were from, and to 'yoyo' diet. I had a conversation with Louise about this: how I'd not wanted to do the health plan because I was worried about my mental health, but I'm glad I took the risk. I was in a better place than I'd ever been; and everyone noticed, which meant that a lot of people I knew wanted to jump on board. They joined the plan, and my business started growing. Within six months, I'd hit my first big promotion.

For the final UK lockdown, from January to March 2021, I decided to make the most of a difficult situation. I set goals and threw myself into fitness rather than sitting on the sofa with Netflix and pizza. I had fun with my new business, embraced work, continued my self-development and mindfulness, and I started looking for a new house to buy.

Oh, and I decided to write a book...!

Epilogue

Over the last couple of years, I've realised just how happy I feel. I've done many incredible things in my 35 years, including the amazing experiences that you've read about in this book, but far more besides. I believe that I've helped a lot of people: through conversations, a hug, some advice or even just a smile. For a while, when I worked as an entertainer, I struggled to see what good my work really brought, but you should never underestimate the value of social contact and making people smile.

Another person who absolutely lived life to its fullest potential was my Grandad, Trevor George. Sadly, he passed into the next world while I was in the process of writing this book. Grandad wanted to reach 100 years but, despite an impressive effort, he fell three years short of this goal. His father had lived to 103, and I think he saw ageing as a competition in the end. I think though, that the question is not 'How long?', but simply 'How?' In his last five years, Grandad did more than a lot of people do in one lifetime. He had a big party in Bournemouth for his 95th birthday, during which he got up to make a speech and danced the night away with his loving family and his vast network of friends. He performed his mentalism act on stage, with Mum, as part of an Olde Tyme Music Hall show. He published his book 'Life, Laughter and Magic' with the help of my cousin, Tom. He took up art as a hobby, and was actually pretty good at it. He even travelled to Ukraine and

Austria to see Tom, as well as his great granddaughter Petra. All this in the last five years! If you want the details of the rest of his full and colourful life, I encourage you to buy his book!

Grandad always inspired me and was my biggest cheerleader. I would visit him at least once a week to share some laughs, stories, achievements or ask for advice. He leaves a massive, Grandad-shaped hole in my world. I am grateful that I was born into a family with so much love and character and that I got to spend lots of time with him.

You've read about my experiences of coping when a loved one had passed. I can assure you, and you will probably know yourself, that it's always different and never pleasant. I am well aware that death is one of my big mental health triggers, but so far, I have not relapsed. I felt more strength this time than I have done before. I believe this is because I am a different person now, thanks to my personal development, counselling and healing over the years.

When Bobe and my paternal Grandad passed over, I was coping with mental health challenges that I'd probably had since I was a child, which had never been dealt with properly. When you are depressed, the smallest thing can tip you over the edge, so a traumatic event like death is bound to cause a massive impact. This time, I am happy within myself, and while I am sad to have lost someone very close to me, it doesn't change my positive sense of wellbeing. I will miss my Grandad every day, in the same way that I miss all my loved ones who have moved on to the next world, but I know they are here in my character too. They are in every thought, every kind word. I wouldn't be who I am today without those who have gone before me. So, I simply feel gratitude towards them.

So, where do I go from here? I don't know. Rather than this disturbing me, I find that it's the most exciting part of life. Doors are always opening, you just have to look for them and walk through them. As a career chameleon I am happy in my current job for now, but I'm never one to turn down an opportunity. I also expect that I'll dance in some way, shape or form, until I drop!

I still feel certain that my 'Why?' in life is to help animals, both human and non-human, so my partner and I have plans to buy some land and start a sanctuary as soon as possible. Picture a two-part kitchen door on a sunny morning, then envisage me opening the top part for a pony to trot up and grab a polo mint. That's absolutely the dream that we intend to make a reality. I appreciate, in the meantime, that every day of my journey is as important as the destination. I believe that whatever life throws me, I must have gratitude for the learning and get back up and move forward.

I hope that this book has given you some excitement for what's to come in your life too, and that it has inspired you to find the courage to be whatever you want to be. The biggest lesson we can all learn is to follow our passions, and to be assured that we can always turn things around.

I encourage you, friends, to go out into the world, be joyful, have fun and shine your light.

Further Information

For more information on body dysmorphic disorder
www.bddfoundation.org

If you are struggling with your mental health, please visit
www.mind.org.uk
www.sane.org.uk

If you would like to explore the vegan lifestyle
www.cowspiracy.com
www.youtube.com/watch?v=UcN7SGGoCNI (Dairy is Scary)
www.whatthehealthfilm.com
www.thesavemovement.org

To support the wonderful charities I've had the pleasure of working with
www.mareandfoal.org
www.rspca-coventryanddistrict.org.uk

For help and support with substance misuse
www.smartrecovery.org.uk
www.alcoholics-anonymous.org.uk

You can find Cilla's dogumentary here
www.youtube.com/watch?v=hEgf_Vczt1o

Credits

Cover Design by Lianna Carnell at South Style Media
www.southstylemedia.co.uk

<u>Front Cover:</u>
Author Photograph - Ami Lauren
Editing – Diane Rees

<u>Back Cover:</u>
Author Photograph – Lucy Fenn
www.lfphotography94.wixsite.com/lucyfenn

<u>Dale Carnegie quote page 13:</u>
https://quotefancy.com/quote/18680

A Word of Thanks...

Mum, for always being my best friend and biggest supporter. Thank you for proof-reading, writing the blurb for the back cover and chatting through anecdotes from my childhood to help with the writing process. I love you so much.

Dad, for being steady and predictable in a world of chaos. Thank you for taking on the role of my Father and excelling at this particular job.

My wider family, past and present. I feel so lucky to have been blessed with a close family within which I feel so much love.

Matthew, although you've not featured in this book, I know we will write 'our story' one day, because it is a beautiful one. Thank you for your love and encouragement.

Shalini, for inspiring me through your dance, mindfulness and your own books. For holding my hand and giving advice throughout the book writing process. For the foreword to this book.

Tom, not only for your editing skills, but for the fun times we have shared throughout our lives, and for the support you have given me in the dark times.

Cilla, my constant companion for eleven beautiful years. Thank you for your unconditional love, for repeatedly saving my life, and for teaching me so many lessons.

Lianna, for your friendship, for introducing Cilla and I to a new community of friends with the 'Devon Dachshund Crew' when we really needed you, and for designing this awesome book cover.

Nem, my partner in crime through the last 25 years. I love you more than you can imagine. Thank you for proof-reading this book.

Jenni, for your friendship, encouragement and laughs, and for proof-reading this book.

The 'So Street' crew, we had the best time, and my wish is that we will dance together again soon. Thank you for providing anecdotes for this book and many, many giggles.

Thanks to all of my employers, past and present, for giving me material.

And finally, thanks to you, the reader. I hope you have enjoyed this book and that you take something from it.

About The Author

Ami Lauren was born into a showbiz family, and grew up amongst entertainers, music, dance and plenty of magic. This gave her an appetite for the different and unusual. From the knowledge and grounding gained during those early years she went on to develop many skills. Her desire for variety and to embrace the numerous different facets of life led her to some interesting careers and experiences along the way and on each occasion she has emerged full of positivity, with a big smile on her face!

Although she was born in Torquay, Devon, Ami has travelled and lived in many different places as she worked across the UK. She set up home for a short while in East London and Stratford-Upon Avon, but returned to settle in her beloved home-town. Ami continues to travel around the globe when possible and truly enjoys this part of life.

Ami's unique and vibrant energy is instrumental in her ongoing work, helping others to achieve or realise their dreams in her own distinctive and expressive manner.

Pen to Published

A 6-month programme that will enable you to
write, publish and promote your book
with Amazon bestselling author Shalini Bhalla-Lucas

You know you have a book in you.
You just don't know how to get it out there...
Let me show you how.

With my Zoom programme you will be able to get your ideas down on paper and be published online on Amazon in SIX months. The programme will keep you focused and accountable – which is what you need when you want to successfully write, publish and promote your book.

I have been trying to write this book for years, but the task seemed enormous and out of reach. Through "Pen to Published", Shalini provided us with the skills and techniques to do so. Under her expert guidance, and with the support of the rest of the first-time authors, writing my book not only became achievable but also one of the most enjoyable experiences of my life. Rosie Miles, Malawi

This is the first time I have been part of a book writing course. I have learned so much from Shalini about how to structure a book by incorporating different writing style approaches and techniques. I am so pleased with the level of support, help and guidance received and would highly recommend "Pen to Published" to anyone who is thinking about writing a book. Joti Gata-Aura, London

For more information about Pen to Published please email
info@justjhoom.co.uk or visit www.justjhoom.co.uk

Printed in Great Britain
by Amazon